ADVANCE PRAISE FOR

White Jesus

"I loved this book! In this interdisciplinary resource, the authors powerfully show that White Jesus isn't an innocuous inaccuracy. Rather, it is a powerful cornerstone of White supremacy and must be seen for the poison that it is. Drawing connections between historical events, theological affirmations and current, real-world examples of White supremacy in Christianity, this book illuminates the many ways in which White Jesus is the enemy, not the savior, of the world. Every Christian influencer—especially clergy, lay leaders, and scholars—should read this book. I know it'll be required reading in the seminary courses I teach for years to come!"

—Christena Cleveland, author of *Disunity in Christ: Uncovering the Hidden Forces That Keep Us Apart*

"For years, I have puzzled over the gaping chasm that so often divides the teachings of Jesus from the practice of White American Christians on matters of race and social justice—a chasm that led Frederick Douglass to affirm in 1845 that 'between the Christianity of this land, and the Christianity of Christ, I recognize the widest possible difference'; a chasm that prompted millions of White American Christians in the 1960s to enroll their children in 'Christian' schools so they could avoid attending school with blacks; and a chasm that, in 2016, allowed some 80% of White evangelical Christians to vote for a man with a long record of racism as president of the United States. This conundrum is so bizarre it simply makes no sense unless we admit to the truth embodied in this book—that we have painted Jesus White, God White, and salvation White. And because our religion is our ultimate concern, we have also painted White the deepest recesses of our hopes, our fears, and our loves. Why then should we be surprised to discover the weeds of racism, deeply rooted and flourishing in the garden of the American church?"

—Richard T. Hughes, author of *Myths America Lives By: White Supremacy and the Stories That Give Us Meaning*

"*White Jesus: The Architecture of Racism in Religion and Education* is a book that deals with the religion of Whiteness and its discontents. A very ambitious text, *White Jesus* seeks to correct the many harms and long-standing traumas that Whiteness as religion has inflicted upon non-White peoples all over the world. Concerned with dismantling White supremacy, it correctly identifies the marriage between Whiteness and Christianity as the starting point for such an endeavor. The authors of this book do an excellent job in dissecting and criticizing the many layers of White religion. From architecture to higher education to missions to liturgy to the ideologies of empire, the historical, cultural, and institutional entanglements of Whiteness and Christianity are laid bare. The gravity of Whiteness and Christianity will force readers to rethink Catholicism, the legacies of the Protestant Reformation, and biblical texts. White audiences, particularly White Christians, who avail themselves to a critique of Whiteness and Christian identity, will be compelled to reimagine Whiteness and Christian identity. *White Jesus* is a timely text that speaks to our contemporary context, where a global resurgence of White nationalism in the United States, Europe, and other parts of the world is reproducing the many problems this book seeks to overcome. I highly recommend *White Jesus*; it is a necessary book for our times."

—Ronald B. Neal, Department for the Study of Religions at Wake Forest University

"Provocative and much needed, this book will probably upset everyone who reads it in some way, which is a good thing—because if we aren't upset, we're probably not paying very much attention."

—Julie J. Park, Associate Professor of Education at the University of Maryland

"In the age of Trump, Americans have allowed a populist jingoism and White supremacy to dominate the conversation on race, even among Christians. American Evangelicals seem to excuse this dysfunctional intersection between a broken culture and God's people. How did we get here? This text provides insight into the blueprint of how this dominating and dominant architecture came into being. By understanding this architecture, we may even have the possibility of plotting a way forward that shirks the White captivity of American Christianity. This work does not allow for simple reductionism, memes, or sound bites. It calls for a critical and intellectual engagement of the topic in ways that could change us. An important and significant contribution to a growing field of study."

—Soong-Chan Rah, Milton B. Engebretson Professor of Church Growth and Evangelism at North Park Theological Seminary and author of *The Next Evangelicalism* and *Prophetic Lament*

"The authors of *White Jesus* have written a book for our time. As Christians, especially in the United States, wrestle with their public witness, this book analyzes the architecture of a theology steeped in Whiteness. It challenges readers to consider how a concept so central to Christianity—salvation by faith in Jesus Christ—can be affected by our socio-cultural location and how it even affects the way we craft material culture to reinforce a racially slanted view of the good news. *White Jesus* should give all of us a certain humility when it comes to theology as we consider the ways we have conflated religion and race and inculcated such ideas through our educational institutions. Although lament is a proper response to this book, so is the sense of hope that comes with realizing that change is possible."

—Jemar Tisby, President of The Witness: A Black Christian Collective

White Jesus

This book is part of the Peter Lang Education list.
Every volume is peer reviewed and meets
the highest quality standards for content and production.

PETER LANG
New York • Bern • Berlin
Brussels • Vienna • Oxford • Warsaw

Alexander Jun, Tabatha L. Jones Jolivet,
Allison N. Ash, & Christopher S. Collins

White Jesus

The Architecture of Racism
in Religion and Education

PETER LANG
New York • Bern • Berlin
Brussels • Vienna • Oxford • Warsaw

Library of Congress Cataloging-in-Publication Data
Names: Jun, Alexander, author. | Jones Jolivet, Tabatha L., author.
Ash, Allison N., author. | Collins, Christopher S., author.
Title: White Jesus: the architecture of racism in religion and education /
Alexander Jun, Tabatha L. Jones Jolivet, Allison N. Ash, and Christopher S. Collins.
Description: New York: Peter Lang, 2018.
Includes bibliographical references and index.
Identifiers: LCCN 2018021043 | ISBN 978-1-4331-5768-4 (hardback: alk. paper)
ISBN 978-1-4331-5769-1 (paperback: alk. paper) | ISBN 978-1-4331-5770-7 (ebook pdf)
ISBN 978-1-4331-5771-4 (epub) | ISBN 978-1-4331-5772-1 (mobi)
Subjects: LCSH: Jesus Christ—Person and offices. | Race awareness.
Race relations—Religious aspects—Christianity.
Racism—Religious aspects—Christianity. | Whites—Race identity.
Christian education.
Classification: LCC BT205 .J86 2018 | DDC 270.089—dc23
LC record available at https://lccn.loc.gov/2018021043
DOI 10.3726/b14191

Bibliographic information published by **Die Deutsche Nationalbibliothek.**
Die Deutsche Nationalbibliothek lists this publication in the "Deutsche
Nationalbibliografie"; detailed bibliographic data are available
on the Internet at http://dnb.d-nb.de/.

For Jeany, Natalia, Isaiah, Jeremiah … and all who have been hurt
by racism in the church
—Alex

For the ancestors, Mom, Dad, and Shelby
—Tabatha

For Jeff, Ellie, and Maddy
—Allison

For Kristy, Mateo, and Adela
—Chris

Any proceeds that would typically go to the authors will be placed
in a scholarship fund for higher education doctoral students at Azusa
Pacific University who are committed to social justice and diversity at
Azusa Pacific University.

TABLE OF CONTENTS

List of Figures   ix
Foreword   xi

Chapter 1. Introduction: The White Architecture of Salvation   1
Chapter 2. White Civil Religion, Empire, and Dominance   17
Chapter 3. How Christianity Became White   29
Chapter 4. The Religious White   41
Chapter 5. White Saviors Proselytizing "Pagans": Missionaries,
           Boarding Schools, and Adoption   55
Chapter 6. Whiteness in Christian Higher Education   71
Chapter 7. White Worship   85
Chapter 8. Before Jesus Became White   99

Afterword   113
Index   117

FIGURES

Figure 1.1: Mural of Jesus   2
Figure 1.2: "Knowledge Over Time" Mural   7
Figure 2.1: American Flag Draped on a Church   25
Figure 5.1: *American Progress* by John Gast   57
Figure A.1: From a Viewing Platform, a Snapshot of the Mural,
             América Tropical, by David Alfaro Siqueiros   115

FOREWORD

We begin this journey by telling our stories. In the following pages each of us explains our experiences and encounters with the topic.

Tabatha L. Jones Jolivet

It is fitting that I (Jones Jolivet) meditate on "White Jesus" and the construction of racism, religion, and education this day, Ash Wednesday. Ash Wednesday customarily follows Mardi Gras, a day often filled with gluttonous traditions that punctuates the end of Carnival season. Today is also the day after U.S. President Donald J. Trump's first address to Congress. I feel the thickness of death suffocating the air we all breathe in the age of Trumpism. Journalist John W. Scheon aptly points out that the message "was a speech full of promise—and promises. And, judging by the number of times President Trump said the word, he followed through on his pledge to put America first."[1] The wisdom of Dr. Maya Angelou helps me to appraise reality: "When someone shows you who they are, believe them the first time."[2] I believe President Trump when he commands chanting crowds with recitations like "Make America great again," for he is appealing to familiar forms of tribalism and nationalism. I am also certain the mythology of White Jesus has gotten

President Trump here, catapulting him to this very moment in the empire's history.

Today, I write as an act of spiritual activism, which leads me to reflect deeply upon not only White Jesus, but also the cross of Jesus of Bethlehem (contemporary Palestine), all the while committing anew to fasting, praying, and almsgiving this Lenten season. It is my annual practice to attend an Ash Wednesday mass, and this year I decided to attend an evening service close to my home. I arrived at a local Catholic church and sat in one of the back pews, which gave me perspective. The parish was filled with people of diverse ethnic backgrounds, and this pleasantly surprised me. The choir and accompanying musicians offered beautiful sacraments of music that reminded me of my grandparents' mass of old, "Lamb of God" and "Mercy, Lord." The homily was a succinctly profound message about the urgency and significance of living what is most important "now." Children and elders alike received the ashes burned from palm branches, and parishioners shared "the peace of the Lord," wet with holy water and illuminated by dimly lit candles. Amid the ashes of our lives and the world, White Jesus commands center stage. Not only does the omnipresence of this symbolic rendering of a cross-hung White Jesus fill the sanctuary and overshadow the tabernacle—where holy communion awaits—this presence pollutes the air like a smog, and my soul aches. Metaphorically and spiritually, I choke like the miner's canary[3] from the noxious gases that threaten to irreparably poison my lungs and the atmosphere we all share. Although a parishioner confessed aloud in prayers of petition the grief of collective sin—racism and xenophobia—White Jesus still threatens the church and the air we breathe. This White Jesus undoubtedly is a fraud, a Sweet'N Low[4] version of Jesus whose life the Gospels recount. The presence of White Jesus is inescapable. Ingesting and maintaining the beliefs, narratives, practices, and institutional investments that are bound to White Jesus is not only hazardous for our collective spiritual health, it is idolatrous. Surely, the "spiritual death" Reverend Martin Luther King, Jr. warned the nation and church about is near. Our saccharin diet leads us here.

Locating Ourselves

We, the authors, ascribe to Christian faith and practice—all the while striving (imperfectly, to be sure) to witness to the cross of Jesus in our everyday lives. We worship in diverse communities of faith, yet equally aspire to embody the same Christian virtues, and we work professionally in Christian colleges and universities. Like members of the Princeton Theological Seminary faculty, we confess our complicity "in the sinful entanglements" that have engineered not only the current sociopolitical terrain,[5] but that also lace the nation's founding and its most treasured institutions—among them, Christian colleges, universities, and churches—many of which are beholden to White Jesus. We confess that we have too long delayed our public critique of the powers and principalities at work in our institutions and lives. We have all too often forgotten that "no institution or government can demand the kind of loyalty that belongs only to God."[6] As we unpack and make sense of the architecture of salvation through racism, religion, and education, we feel compelled to locate ourselves in the conversation by revealing salient dimensions of our social group identities that shape how we "see" the world.

I (Jones Jolivet) attribute to my ancestors and parents an early religious formation in Christian belief and practice. Their living faith was a cocoon for me, and I consider their transmission of spiritual wealth my greatest inheritance. As a small toddler, I can vividly remember my paternal grandmother, Lola Jolivet, giving me a set of pale-pink rosary beads and kneeling with me to pray the "Lord's Prayer" before bedtime. This made spirituality real to me at an early age. I grew up in Houston and Austin, Texas in the U.S. South and came of age in the 1970s and 1980s at a time when critical victories achieved during the modern civil rights movement were newfound. My parents and their parents before them had lived in all-Black communities (which they treasured) under the system of U.S. apartheid and racial control—its contemporary manifestations still at work in insidious ways today.[7] Both sets of my grandparents were Black Catholics, and so were my parents until they began attending an all-Black Church of Christ—an eccentric, post-Enlightenment religious movement that prized Scripture as the normative source of truth and revelation, a "blueprint" for salvation.[8] Like Catholics at the time, members of Churches of Christ believed they were the only Christians. My immediate family had overnight gone from being occasional Catholics to devout believers. We religiously followed the "five acts" of worship in Scripture, and proselytized others with the "Plan of Salvation" that had been "made plain" in Sunday school, Sunday morning and evening worship, Wednesday night Bible classes, tracts, and gospel meetings. The "blueprint" of salvation—the path to eternal life with God—came as a result of hearing, believing, repenting, confessing, and being baptized … in a Church of Christ alone. While I never encountered renderings of White Jesus in a Church of Christ setting (like I had observed in mass), I still experienced the ominous logic of Whiteness in the traditions of my all-Black church. White dominance functioned in our traditions, practices, and interpretations of Scripture to constrain our spiritual imagination and experience of God.

I remember being baptized at a gospel meeting at Fifth Ward Church of Christ in Houston, where Jack Evans, Sr.[9] was a guest revivalist and prominent preacher among the circuit of Black male evangelists in Churches of Christ. After listening to Evans' sermon, being saved was urgent in my ten-year-old mind and confessing that Jesus Christ was the son of God and being baptized ("before Jesus returned") seemed reasonable. Remarkably, I was awake during worship (I was prone to falling asleep during long services). At the "invitation," I jumped from my seat to be baptized—and it never occurred to me that I should obtain my parents' consent. My salvation was on the line, and I needed to secure my spot in heaven. The hymns we sang from the red book in our a capella tradition have never left me: "Just as I am without one plea, but that Thy blood was shed for me. And that thou bid me come to Thee. O, Lamb of God I come. Will you come to the fountain free? Will you come, 'Tis for you and me; Thirsty soul, hear the welcome call. There's a fountain open for all. Praise the Lord, Salvation has been brought down."[10]

The religious and cultural influences of the Black Catholic church and Black Churches of Christ shape who I am today and inform my epistemological scaffold. I self-identify as a Black woman from the U.S. South, who navigates what Patricia Hill Collins describes as the interlocking nature of oppression, especially within academic institutions.[11] As an "insider-outsider" to academe, my critical faith witness is grounded in the Black prophetic tradition, most especially intersectional Womanist thought and praxis.[12] I also benefit from the enormous advantage I derive from privileged dimensions of my identity. I am heterosexual, middle class, able-bodied, documented, and highly educated. In my professional life, I have worked in White-dominant Christian universities. For this reason, I am actively engaged in a decolonizing project.

Alexander Jun

Born to a foreign news correspondent covering the White House for a South Korean newspaper in the 1960s, I grew up with my father regaling me with stories of life in the foreign press corps. It was a time in the United States when the cultural and social climate was shifting. Note that it was the mid-1960s and a travel ban was in effect for undesirable poor countries. Well before the Muslim ban and references to shithole countries by the 45th president, people from my heritage country of South Korea were not welcome in the United States. Only in 1965 did the U.S. lift immigration restrictions for Asian countries, where only a decade previously refugees from the same war-torn Korean nation sought entry onto American shores. My late father had never expressed any particular interest in church, much to the chagrin of my maternal grandmother, who prayed for his salvation every day. My mother, who grew up in Seoul, Korea, was raised Roman Catholic—but, growing up, I never saw her or my father attend church. Much later in my adult life, I learned that my mother, who faithfully attended mass and Bible study as a young woman, stopped going to church and ostensibly walked away from her faith after joining her husband in America. The reason, as it turned out, was the racism she experienced in the Catholic church, as well as in Washington, DC and the surrounding areas. I have always wanted to know specific examples of happened, but have been too afraid to ask. Regardless, her experiences were so negative that they drove her to walk away from God's people. How did God's people (mis)represent love and community for her?

As an unchurched child growing up, I "got saved" my first year in college through a campus outreach ministry by and for ethnic Koreans, called Korean Campus Mission. My first church experience was at a Korean Full Gospel church in Koreatown, near downtown Los Angeles. Most of the 3,000-member church's worship services were conducted in Korean. My first encounter with White Jesus also occurred at this church. I found it odd that at such a predominantly ethnic Korean church, iconic velvet photos of White Jesus with long flowing brown hair and beautiful blue eyes were visible on the walls of Sunday School classrooms as well as in the sanctuary of the church.

Upon graduating college, I found that Reformed theology and Presbyterianism was a much better fit doctrinally and theologically for me. Where the Pentecostal faith tradition relied heavily on the life in the spirit, Presbyterians found the life of the mind more palatable, while holding on to my close connection to the work of the Holy Spirit. I embrace my hybridity and refer to myself as Presbycostal. In the summer of 1993, I had the privilege of helping to plant a small Korean Presbyterian church in Southern California with spiritual co-laborers from my days in college ministry; I am still actively involved at this church today. In addition to serving my local church for the past quarter-century, I have also been quite actively involved in my denomination, the Presbyterian Church in America (PCA). I consider it a tremendous

honor to be have able to engage in conversations around race in my denomination in the last few years; much of our efforts led to a public and corporate
repentance for past racial sins of commission and omission during the civil
rights era.[13]

Spiritually, I identify as Reformed and Presbyterian. Some people have
tried to insult me by calling me a Calvinist; at times I wore this as a badge of
honor, and at other times I was ashamed for the way my theology had been
used to spiritually bully and abuse others. Having served as a Ruling Elder for
my local church for fifteen years, I also became more actively involved at the
national level of the PCA, and was elected as the 45th Moderator (kind of a
big deal if you are Presbyterian) in 2017.

With the election, I became the first Asian American to become a moderator. Finding myself atop my denominational food chain has been eye-opening
to say the least. What has become more abundantly clear in my interactions
with various groups and individuals in my denomination is that, in order to
be a good churchman, I need to think White. Code-shifting never ends for
me, and the socialization process requires that I understand and embrace
White logic. While I too embrace all the creeds, confessions, and the beloved
Roberts Rules of Order that my denominational elders hold dear, I had never
questioned the cultural roots embedded in what I simply considered normative theology and doctrine. I resonate with the words of Cornel West, that I
am also trying to kill the white supremacy that lives in me.

The publication of our (Collins and Jun) first book, *White Out*, was met
with mixed reviews within my White denominational family, with the greatest
resistance, fear, and criticism coming from a fringe element of ultra-conservative
White brothers and sisters. I call them my brothers and sisters because that is
what they are to me. The blood of Jesus unites us and I love them. Theologically,
we align in many ways, but the biggest area of contention is along the lines of
race, ethnicity, and racial justice. Many of the White brothers and sisters have
become the biggest source of encouragement to me. May we collectively pursue
racial reconciliation as one spiritual family.

Allison N. Ash

Some of my earliest childhood memories of church include watching the
annual parade of ten-year-olds walk to the front of the church to receive their
very own Bibles. My small-town Midwest church ritualized this experience as
each child came of age, and when I walked forward to receive my gold-covered

Good News Bible in front of our church, I believed that book was one of the most important gifts I had ever received. I began privately reading it … every night. However, when I read one particular passage in the Old Testament that referenced children being punished for the sins of their parents, that book no longer seemed like good news. Around the time that I received my Bible, my parents had gotten divorced, so when I read this verse, I couldn't help but conclude that the "sin of my parents" was divorce, and I would be punished for it. In my young mind, there was nothing I could do to escape God's punishment; my parents had determined my fate.

After I shared with a school mentor my fledgling theological concerns, she told me that I needed to have a "personal relationship" with Jesus and be "born again"—I simply needed to say a prayer to accept Jesus as my savior; Jesus had taken care of all those things I was reading in the Old Testament. My mentor's language was different than what I had heard at my church. People in my church did not use terms like being "born again" and having a "personal relationship" with Jesus. We were the *liberal* church in town because we built houses for the poor and embraced Vietnamese refugees in the 1970s. Walking bags of canned goods to the altar as our offering and giving my extra pairs of shoes to child refugees were commonplace activities. As the church choir director's daughter, the church building was my home away from home—a place where I built forts in the choir loft, played hide-and-seek in the organ chambers, and generally felt a sense of community and belonging. However, after praying the prayer that my mentor encouraged me to pray, I believed that my church had failed me. They had taught me to care about the needs of others but not about my own risk of eternal punishment. This spiritual and doctrinal conundrum is one that I see among many Christians in my circles. People ask, what is more important: one's eternal destiny or seeking justice in the world? Who was right … my church or my mentor?

My answer to this question, which demonstrates my particular positionality, can be found in my adherence to two worlds that many would believe to be political enemies—evangelicalism and social justice. As an evangelical, I believe that the prayer my mentor encouraged me to pray was a significant and critical moment in my spiritual life and fundamental to the "Good News" of Christianity. As someone committed to social justice, I understand that the kinds of acts of care and service that I witnessed and participated in as a child in my church were deeply spiritual and rooted in the work and teachings of Jesus. In my theological, spiritual, and epistemological world, having one without the other is an incomplete faith.

Even though I eventually attended churches that were vastly different from one another and emphasized different sides of this theological equation, the churches had two things in common: they were almost completely White, and the pastors never preached about race or racial justice. In my churches, Jesus was White.

What it meant that I was White (or my presumption that Jesus was White) had escaped my self-reflection until I learned about my family's racial heritage later in life. My mother's family members were from England and Germany and my father's family members were of African descent, Native American, and Dutch. In his hometown community, my father's family was part Black, but he passed as White after going to college. As I was growing up, we never spoke about the racial heritage of either side of my family. However, I would later learn that racial wounds had scarred my father and his family: the kinds of wounds that occur when trying to be White with dark skin in a White community, a White community that made the rules about who could do things like rent apartments and freely ride on public transportation without being arrested; rules that my family tried to obey by hiding their dark skin whenever possible. I have these generational wounds of racism inside of me—the teachings from a White society that told my family that Black was inferior, a teaching that was like a tornado of shame, ripping its way through souls and families. I have been in the path of this tornado's destruction while seeing and feeling the effects of racist wounds from those who believed this lie of shame. But my White skin painted for me a different story, a story of unrealized privilege and opportunity that separated me—in the most salient of ways—from my Black relatives and connected me to the White side of my family.

As a White person committed to racial justice, I understand the complexities associated with such a position. I believe that I will always be on a trajectory of discovering the ways that my mind has been formed in a society and church that was founded on and intermingled with White supremacy. The process of becoming aware of the realities of race, privilege, and power is, for me, a process that will likely never have an ending. At times, in my efforts to seek change and justice, I, ironically, have the potential to demonstrate my privilege by exercising power over others in unjust ways. Understanding privilege without surrendering power can be its own form of injustice. These are the kinds of complexities that I expect to be discovering and seeking to dismantle inside of myself for the rest of my life; a process that is critical to undergo as I seek the kind of justice that I believe Jesus sought in his life and teachings on earth.

Christopher S. Collins

During the Civil War, my great-great-Grandfather Tomlin was captured twice while fighting for the Confederate army. Some time after that, his family clan and a couple of other families in Lamar County, Alabama signed a charter for the beginning of the Ole Liberty Church of Christ. The single-room chapel was built in the 1860s, and adjacent to the building is a cemetery where many of my ancestors are buried. Ole Liberty was born out of a "back to the Bible" movement that spread across the South in the late-nineteenth century. I do not know how this particular movement connected with my family more than 150 years ago. Perhaps it was while some of the soldiers were at war, or perhaps a traveling preacher came through with a message that resonated in that area. Whatever it was, the message took root deeply enough to leave me with a religious tradition that stays with my family even today—primarily because of the women in that family line.

What has particularly stuck with me is a figure in that movement that embodied some counter-cultural beliefs—David Lipscomb. He lived in Nashville, opposed slavery, worked across religious lines to help people who were poor and sick, was a pacifist, and generally opposed involvement with the military and government civic affairs. He exhibited a deep belief in a Jesus who conveyed, "you cannot serve two masters," "we are citizens of one kingdom," and "render unto the emperor what is the emperor's [taxes] and unto God what is God's [faith and loyalty]." Ironically, as this movement became less sectarian and more acceptable to a society that valued civil religion, it maintained a literal approach to the Bible and lived by the saying, "speak where the Bible speaks and be silent where the Bible is silent." The more civil religion and patriotism came to dominate the movement, the more Whitewashed Jesus became. The literal approach to the Bible concerned Sunday morning dogma, not loving enemies and taking care of the sick, imprisoned, and needy. My religious identity is in tandem with that post-political, primitive form of following Jesus.

My Dad preached in many churches and gospel meetings in sometimes hot and quaint rural churches across the South. I first came into contact with the image of a White Jesus that was printed on fans tucked behind pews and used by glistening older women in country churches in Alabama, Tennessee, Louisiana, Kansas, and Texas. What I realize now is that I encountered the meaning of White Jesus long before I saw that image.

White Jesus

In this book, we conceive White Jesus as a socially constructed apparatus—a mythology that animates the architecture of salvation—that operates stealthily as a veneer for patriarchal White supremacist, capitalist, and imperialist sociopolitical, cultural, and economic agendas. White Jesus was constructed by combining empire, colorism, racism, education, and religion—and the byproduct is a distortion that reproduces violence in epistemic and physical ways. We distinguish White Jesus from Jesus of the Gospels, the one whose life, death, and resurrection demands sacrificial love as a response—a love ethic, to be sure—the kind the Prophet Isaiah instructs Hebrew people to follow in chapter 1, verse 17:[14]

> learn to do good;
> seek justice,
>   rescue the oppressed,
> defend the orphan,
>   plead for the widow. (Isaiah 1:17 NRSV)

Practicing this kind of love ethic is countercultural to adherents of the nation's civil religion because the mythology of White Jesus is so pervasive—and its proselytizing power is akin to snake oil peddling. White Jesus, after all, cannot simply be reduced to iconography or impotent symbolism. What is more, White Jesus must be understood as more than mere anthropomorphism—that is, making God like us—much like the White Jesus I (Jones Jolivet) encountered during Ash Wednesday mass. Instead, White Jesus is a prevailing mythology that functions to reinscribe the patriarchal White supremacist, capitalist, imperialist agendas that conceived the nation and "stamped"[15] its institutions at their inception. This mythology maintains the social order and provides a sacred framework as cover for the sociopolitical, historical, cultural, economic, ideological, and anthropological investments of the empire and its social institutions. White Jesus is a fraudulent scheme that, like many devotees of Jesus of Bethlehem, I (Jones Jolivet) naively fell for. I confess that I not only believed the lies of the snake oil peddler, but I failed to notice them at work in everyday life, including the ways I maintained them. This book is about naming the lies, reclaiming the person of Jesus, and reasserting a vision of power that locates Jesus of the Gospels in solidarity with the easily disposed. The catalytic, animating, life-altering power of the cross of Jesus is enough to subdue White Jesus and his patronage. In doing so, we hope that in the death of White Jesus, the new life that Jesus of the Gospels brings will be done "on earth as it is in heaven."[16]

About the Cover

The cover is a combination of two images. On the left is a painting that has been reproduced many times. It is a White Jesus that is widely distributed. A review of images of Jesus shows indications of black and brown skin and corresponding features for centuries until Constantine made Christianity openly acceptable in the early fourth century. The images of Jesus then began to reflect the character of empire. There were still some depictions of a darker Jesus until around the thirteenth and fourteenth centuries in the Common Era, when almost all of the images turned European. The Whitewashing process occurred over centuries.[17] Now, the blending of image and empire have imprinted this constructed White Jesus onto the image and identity of the church and Christians around the world for centuries.

The right side of the image is a rendition of a drawing from the journal of a young White man who committed a heinous crime of White supremacist violence. On June 17, 2015, a group of faithful Black followers of Jesus gathered in the historic "Mother Emanuel" African Methodist Episcopal Church in Charleston, SC. The man entered the meeting and less than an hour later shot and murdered the following people:

Cynthia Hurd, 54
Susie Jackson, 87
Ethel Lance, 70
Depayne Middleton-Doctor, 49
The Rev. Clementa Pinckney, 41
Tywanza Sanders, 26
The Rev. Daniel Simmons, 74
The Rev. Sharonda Coleman-Singleton, 45
Myra Thompson, 59[18]

The perpetrator was arrested. While in prison, he drew the image of White Jesus in his journal. But, the imprint of White Jesus manifested long before he drew this picture. The journal also included the note, "There is plenty of evidence to indicate that Christianity can be a [sic] warriors of religion."[19] Our purpose in writing this short book is to put together that evidence, and to show it as an aberration of the radical Jesus recorded in the New Testament.

Notes

1. John W. Schoen points out that Trump used the phrase "America" (or another variation of the term) seventy times throughout the speech. Source: Retrieved from http://www.cnbc.com/2017/03/01/trumps-speech-to-congress-puts-america-first-dozens-of-times.html

2. Podrazik, Joan. "WATCH: Avoid A Big Relationship Mistake With One Of Oprah's Favorite Life Lessons." The Huffington Post. March 14, 2013. Accessed July 09, 2018. https://www.huffingtonpost.com/2013/03/14/oprah-life-lesson-maya-angelou_n_2869235.html

3. In *The Miner's Canary: Enlisting Race, Resisting Power, Transforming Democracy*, Lani Guinier and Gerald Torres attribute to Felix Cohen (1953) the assertion, "Like the miner's canary, the Indian marks the shift from fresh air to poison gas in our political atmosphere, and our treatment of the Indian … marks the rise and fall in our democratic faith." They go on to write, "we hope to show that Cohen's canary is not alone. All canaries bear watching. Our democratic future depends on it" (located just before the prologue).

4. Sweet'N Low is a trademark brand of saccharin, an artificial sweetener that bears the warning label: "Use of this product may be hazardous to your health. This product contains saccharin, which has been determined to cause cancer in laboratory animals." Source: Retrieved from https://www.cancer.gov/about-cancer/causes-prevention/risk/diet/artificial-sweeteners-fact-sheet

5. On February 24, 2017, faculty at Princeton Theological Seminary released a statement condemning "the god of Donald Trump's 'America first' nationalism," and distinguishing this "god" from the "God revealed in our scriptures." Source: Retrieved from http://www.ptsem.edu/news/faculty-statement

6. Princeton Theological Seminary faculty statement. Retrieved from http://www.ptsem.edu/news/faculty-statement

7. For further explication of contemporary forms of racial control, such as mass incarceration, see Bryan Stevenson's *Just Mercy*, Michelle Alexander's *The New Jim Crow*, and Ava DuVernay's documentary film *13th*.

8. In 1996 and later in 2001, Richard T. Hughes published two authoritative histories of Churches of Christ, describing the tradition at large as "a promising frontier movement that burst with great vitality onto the American religious scene in the early nineteenth century" (p. 3). Most notably, Hughes (2001) asserts, "Building on a radically sectarian message that proclaimed themselves the one true church, Churches of Christ won hundreds and thousands of converts in the 1920s, 1930s, and 1940s, then capitalized on the post-World War II religious revival to enhance their numerical base even further" (p. 3). Both books, as Hughes asserts (1996) are "principally about the white mainstream Churches of Christ that traces its American heritage to Barton W. Stone and Alexander Campbell in the early nineteenth century and that, in the twentieth century, has thrived especially in a region running from Middle Tennessee to West Texas."

9. Founder and then-president, Southwestern Christian College.

10. *Sacred Selections for the Church* (54th edition).

11. See *Black Feminist Thought*, Patricia Hill Collins (2000).

12. Patricia Hill Collins writes about the marginal status Black women occupy in academe and the agency we employ in this context to produce Black Feminist thought as creative expressions of activism. *Black Prophetic Fire*, Cornel West in dialogue with and edited by Christa Buschendorf (2014).
13. Retrieved from http://www.christianitytoday.com/news/2016/june/pca-apologizes-for-new-and-old-racism.html.
14. See bell hooks and Cornel West's discussions of "love ethic."
15. In "Stamped from the Beginning: The Definitive History of Racist Ideas in America," Ibram X. Kendi documents the myriad of ways that the construction of the United States as a nation is rooted in racist ideas.
16. The Lord's Prayer is attributed to Jesus in the Gospel of Matthew 6:9–13 King James Version (KJV).
17. See "Jesus Image Gallery: What Did Jesus Look Like?" *Religion Facts*. Retrieved March 1, 2018 from http://www.religionfacts.com/jesus/gallery, and King, Shaun. "Jesus depictions today further promote a white supremacist agenda," *Daily News*, December 23, 2015. Retrieved from https://www.nydailynews.com/amp/news/national/king-white-jesus-symbol-u-s-anglo-saxon-agenda-article-1.2475220.
18. NPR Staff. June 18, 2015. "The Victims: 9 Were Slain at Charleston's Emanuel AME Church." Retrieved April 2, 2018 from https://www.npr.org/sections/thetwo-way/2015/06/18/415539516/the-victims-9-were-slain-at-charlestons-emanuel-ame-church
19. Hawes, Jennifer Berry. January 5, 2017. "Dylann Roof Jailhouse Journal," *The Post and Courier*. Retrieved February 5, 2018 from https://www.postandcourier.com/dylann-roof-jailhouse-journal/pdf_da3e19b8-d3b3-11e6-b040-03089263e67c.html

· 1 ·

INTRODUCTION

The White Architecture of Salvation

The cross and the lynching tree are separated by nearly 2,000 years ... both are symbols of death, one represents a message of hope and salvation, while the other signified the negation of that message by white supremacy ... What is at stake is the credibility and promise of the Christian gospel.

—James H. Cone, *The Cross and the Lynching Tree*[1]

Introduction

At a dominantly White evangelical Christian university in southern California, a mural of White Jesus holding out a Bible stands thirty feet tall. The mural was painted on the side of a building many years ago and has been restored to preserve its place on campus. When prospective students have toured the campus and walked by the mural, tour guides have reportedly pointed out that Jesus' skin color is the same as the pages of the Bible—an image reflecting "the Word became flesh" (referencing the biblical passage in John 1:14). This explanation may help to distract people touring the university from the controversy surrounding an oversized White Jesus towering over people while holding the Bible (which, ironically, Jesus never actually held). The mural has provoked a variety of discussions and has been reported as a source of deep pain and exclusion. When the Word becomes flesh, it begs the question, what color is flesh? Historically, Jesus was a Jewish man of Middle Eastern descent who was born into a social hierarchy that assigned him a low socioeconomic status. This book explores how Jesus and Christianity became White in many different periods and places, and what the socially constructed mythology of White Jesus means in the context of a diverse, multicultural, and global society.

Figure 1.1: Mural of Jesus.
Source: "Bible, Jesus, Mural, Biola, Christian, Church," *Pixaby,* last modified on March 25, 2014, https://pixabay.com/en/bible-jesus-mural-painting-biola-295735/.

The university's mural has withstood great scrutiny and was even publicly defended by its president, who committed to maintaining the mural in its current form in 2010, while also establishing other places on campus to have dialogue and more multicultural representations. In 2013, the president published a letter explaining more about his decision to keep the mural and how it evolved, including the justification:

> I made the decision because I struggled with how to articulate the mural's removal
> to those in our broader constituency who love and support Biola because we're

unashamed to have a bigger-than-life Jesus mural on our wall. These included alumni, supporters, parents and trustees, among others. The symbolism of the Jesus mural to many was that Biola remained Christ-centered and biblically faithful. I knew that for them, if Jesus came down or were painted over, it could be seen as Biola moving away from its moorings, even though this was not true. I thought then that no matter how hard I tried to explain why I called for the painting to be painted over, it could be seen as the new president's agenda to erode our deepest convictions, to head down the slippery slope.[2]

In addition, the president made reference to the mural artist's other works, namely *111th Street Jesus*. The mural of Jesus that was located on 111th street in downtown Los Angeles was positioned much closer to the eye level of the viewer, and Jesus was rendered with arms wide open—and with an appearance that was more reflective of the brown people living in the surrounding community. It is almost as though the two murals by the same muralist reflect the communities in which they were embedded. Unfortunately, the 111th Street Jesus mural was painted over in 1999 by the owner of the liquor store on which it appeared. The irony that White Jesus was restored on an evangelical university campus and that the brown Jesus in Los Angeles was whitewashed is symbolic of the narrative we explore in this book.

Although the two renderings of Jesus may reflect the differences of the communities in which they are situated, the same artist painted them. Observing the racial differences in the depictions of Jesus is an appropriate entry point to understanding the Whitening of Jesus. In churches, educational institutions, and throughout society, the power of White normativity persists, and Jesus' Whiteness matters. For example, the Huffington Post[3] and other news organizations reported public outrage and shock that the Great Mall of America would feature Black Santa for the first time in 2016. While some may describe Santa without the qualifier of skin color, the rampant sense of shock about Black Santa reveals how White normativity works to reproduce White supremacy. Santa Claus is assumed to be White until someone suggests he is not. Contesting Santa's Whiteness illustrates this illogical sequence. When Fox News host Megyn Kelly discussed an article that insinuated how iconography is a powerful tool of White normativity (like in the case of Santa), Kelly objected to the argument's absurdity:

> Jesus was a white man, too. It's like we have, he's a historical figure that's a verifiable fact, as is Santa, I just want kids to know that. How do you revise it in the middle of the legacy in the story and change Santa from white to black?[4]

From the walls of institutions to the words of journalists and commentators on nationally-syndicated circuits, Jesus is perpetually depicted as White. This matters. White Jesus is a reflection of a historical scaffolding of dominance in the construction of knowledge, legitimacy, power, and ownership, and its construction has been and is being protected by a sacred canopy—a theological expression of White dominance. Put in more erudite terms, "The theological meanings invested in epidermal appearances served in the function of the exploitation of both (indigenous) native and (imported) slave labor for European colonial and later imperial enterprises." We will explore this in the following sections and chapters.[5]

Although paintings at universities and racial depictions of Santa Claus may seem superficial, we believe that they represent part of the fabric that has generated a simultaneous defense of Christianity and White dominance through a commitment to President Donald Trump. The newfound zeal embedded in White supremacists marching in Charlottesville and inciting violence is not disconnected from the extensive claims that Trump has been sent by God to protect the Christian interests of the United States of America. The intersection of these two events are a reflection of the ongoing construction of salvation from a dominant White perspective.

The White Architecture of Salvation

This book is a companion to *White Out: Understanding White Privilege and Dominance in the Modern Age*, which explained the concept:

> The White architecture of the mind is a term and an analogy to highlight that the mind is a result of a set of blueprints, constructions, walls, doors, windows, and pathways that influence and predispose individuals to react based on a systemic logic that was socially constructed.[6]

In *White Jesus*, we expand the concept of the White architecture of the mind to explore the White architecture of salvation. As an explanatory tool, the White architecture of salvation illuminates the role of White supremacy and domination in prescribing who is accepted, legitimized, and powerful—hence, rationalizing who is chosen, set apart, and saved. In this book, we argue that the logic of the White architecture of salvation buttresses the forms of enduring material and symbolic violence at work in the world. So what is White Jesus? It is a symbol that is visible in paintings, photos, depictions, and mythologies surrounding the physical interpretation of the person of Jesus. There is a salient and underlying logic behind the symbol of a Jesus who looks Anglo Saxon. The Whiteness of Jesus is a manifestation of the White architecture of salvation—which is itself the manifestation of a god-like White supremacy infused with the power to define what it means to have immortality, or in Christian lingo, to be *saved*.

Because we believe that reality is socially constructed,[7] we recognize that understanding of salient concepts like salvation is also socially constructed. Salvation functions to preserve, rescue, or save from harm or ruin. In Christian theology, Jesus is the savior and the harm is sin, an immoral thought or action dictated by divine law and a system of power and principalities. Here, we explore how these concepts are socially constructed and understood through religiously-sanctioned White dominance. As authors, we hold a variety of beliefs about Christian salvation, and our beliefs are evolving, under construction, fallible—hence, manifestations of our own faith systems. Our beliefs, however, are not the principal subject of this book. Our primary concern is how systems of salvation are socially constructed through White dominance, which has infected our own understanding. We strive to bring epistemic humility to the project.

In explorations of social issues and theology, James Cone extended the question: "What is the connection between the dominant material relations and the ruling theological ideas in a given society?"[8] Cone included that thinking about the sacred must not be divorced from our actual lives. We adopt this assertion as fundamental to our examination and confess our own limitations and intentions. Following Cone, we know that we will confront and confess our limitations and "inability to say anything about God which is not at the same time a statement about the social context of [our] own existence."[9] Furthermore, we acknowledge the predicament of attempts to assert fundamental objectivity. The appearance of objectivity does not replace the need for theological explanation, nor religion with science. The appearance of objectivity, instead, replaces God with the scientist.

The White architecture of salvation, then, is a prequel or predecessor to the White architecture of the mind, which likely evolved into a mature ideology during the Enlightenment period. Preoccupation with rationality during the Enlightenment replaced theological explanations with the scientific method—namely, steps that included observation and rigid formalized testing—leaving the researcher and person interpreting the results with a sense of objectivity. Enlightenment hyperrationality was not only an attempt to replace God or the perceived superstitious belief systems embedded with religion; it was an attempt to be God. Adherents to positivism asserted that through systems of analysis using the scientific method, knowledge was immutable and objective. In essence, human beings could view the world with God-like eyes and know the world with an omniscient mind. If scientists verified and produced knowledge using empirical methods, then knowledge production could bestow deified status. By the 1700s, "the theological coagulation of 'white' and 'right,' 'light' and 'might,' began to gain ontological voice ... Enlightenment philosophers and natural sciences supplied the map."[10]

— Prior to the Enlightenment, different religious belief systems held normative epistemic power. In the historical arc between Judaism and Christianity, for example, if something went wrong with God's people, the explanatory approach was to examine humanity's relationship with God. This approach was evident in the Holy Bible, the first part of which is the Hebrew Bible. Christians consider the second part, the New Testament, as God's fulfillment of messianic promises in the Old Testament. The New Testament depicts the life and teachings of Jesus in his first-century, earthly role. Moving from those early teachings of Jesus, one important chapter in the book traces, historically, how Christianity became White.

One way to understand the historical evolution of the White architecture of salvation is to examine a thirty-foot wall mural, "Knowledge over Time," located at another dominantly White evangelical Christian university. A grant-funded project, the ceramic mural was created in conjunction with members of the university community and local middle school children. The mural illustrates a timeline of "significant" events in human history, and throughout the timeline, God's immanence and activity in the world is visible. The mural begins with a partial imitation of Michelangelo's "Creation of Adam," a fresco painting located in the Sistine Chapel in Vatican City, which memorializes the Judeo-Christian creation narrative. For viewers familiar with Michelangelo's painting and socialized to accept, prima facie, the canonized ideology of Eurocentric liberal arts education, the mural evokes the depiction of a Judeo-Christian God, whose Whiteness and maleness is categorically normalized. God's White hand stretches toward Adam's and infuses life into human existence. The mural contains other depictions of human knowledge and progress, which are accentuated by Holy Scripture and Christian religious events. Interwoven are symbols, such as the cross of Jesus, which function not only to signify Jesus' death, but to legitimize the timeline's events with epistemological dominance.

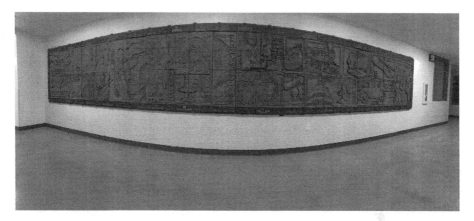

Figure 1.2: "Knowledge Over Time" Mural.
Source: The College of Music and the Arts sponsored by the Azusa Pacific University Libraries. Photo Credit: Christopher S. Collins.

With the exception of a single image representing Egyptian civilization in North Africa, etched into the mural is a direct geographical line of knowledge that is traced from Europe to North America and conveys God-ordained authority and legitimacy. While viewing the progression of images and ideas over time may be considered normative to someone casually passing by, the ideology carved into the wall, curricula, psyche, and construction of salvation is one that assumes and reinforces a white Euro-American line of knowledge production that is God-ordained and objective—what dominant academe considers the highest order of thinking. By contrast, the mural conceals the theft of knowledge, illegal land acquisition, violent relocations, systematic removal, genocide, and enslavement, which occurred in the name of this Western European-North American line of knowledge production—under the auspices of God and progress. The mural blends together portrayals of the pre-Enlightenment and Enlightenment eras, which is key to constructing the White architecture of salvation. Building universal and seemingly objective knowledge with a God-like point of view, Western epistemology—including Christian theology, secular philosophy, and Enlightenment/post-Enlightenment science—pretends to be independent of geography and history. Through images of God and systems of knowledge production, the White architecture of salvation reinforces beliefs in the superiority of White men living in Europe and North America and the salvific power of their empire-building projects.

The West is at the center of epistemic articulation, where White society believes knowledge was conceived. From a Eurocentric perspective, the rest of the world was an object to be described, studied, and objectified. For the purposes of this book, the West is also the source and principal driver of the White architecture of salvation. As seen along the ceramic mural, the God-knowledge-progress continuum begins with God's hands and ends with "man" walking on the moon. It is interesting to observe that the person walking on the moon has two grenades attached to a space suit, which is historically inaccurate. Although no one carried a grenade onto the moon, the role of militarization and nation-state violence—in the name of the God, knowledge, and progress—is central to the construction of the White architecture of salvation, which is a racist mythology that is rooted in particular geohistorical, geopolitical, and geoeconomic social conditions.

Perhaps a current manifestation of this continuum is the 2016 election of Donald J. Trump as the 45th president of the United States. This victory was achieved with the overwhelming support of White evangelical voters. Exit polls showed that 80%[11] or 4 in 5 White evangelical voters selected Trump.[12] The numbers speak volumes, whether White evangelicals voted *for* Trump or *against* Hillary Clinton. The data also expose an ongoing myth that to be truly Christian you must be White, American, and Republican. This equation is indicative of a foreclosed social group identity that cannot be dismantled without great emotional and psychological pain.

In higher education, and Christian higher education in particular, we continue to witness the geopolitics of knowledge production and the dominance of the Western university throughout the world. In this book, we will examine the convergence of the White architecture of the mind and the White architecture of salvation through the historical development of White Jesus, the missionary work of European, Western European, and North American industrialized countries to the rest of the world, and the ways in which systems of schooling were leveraged as tools. We trace the geographical and biographical origins of White Jesus and explicate the White architecture of salvation.

White missionaries delivered a consistent message to places around the rest of the world—ones they deemed less knowledgeable, less rational, and less objective: that religion (and Christianity in particular) is central to how salvation is achieved. Salvation is not simply a religious proposition or even a belief system. Instead, it is language, behavior, and accepted ways of thinking about the world which form an ontology and hierarchy of knowledge. While there are many familiar examples, we have an important chapter that explores how European and North American missionaries around the world required that English be spoken and banned cultural practices, languages, dancing, rituals, relationship patterns, and so on. These important historical examples of the White architecture of salvation are especially problematic in the contemporary setting, since practices of cultural domination and exploitation are associated with systems of slavery.

The White architecture of salvation was not simply a mythology that existed. Rather, Whites who espoused to be Christian exploited the Bible to justify slavery and other forms of domination to reinforce their power and status in the social hierarchy. Therefore, the White architecture of salvation is the historical, geographical, economic, and biographical foundation upon which White Jesus was constructed and continues to exist as implicit knowledge to some, which explains salvation, religion, and knowledge as something obvious. Contesting Jesus' Whiteness not only threatens the visual and anthropomorphic depictions of Jesus, but also exposes the foundation upon which White Jesus was constructed and that sustains the White architecture of salvation. If White Jesus is the "theological muscle of the power structure of the color line and its global manifestations: colonization, imperialism, national, and white terrorism in America,"[13] then the White architecture of salvation is the logic by which those who do not fall under the White sacred canopy can be saved, redeemed, and justified through subservience to White domination, authority, and power. Redemption under this scheme requires assimilation and/or annihilation—physically, mentally, emotionally, spiritually, epistemologically, and ontologically. The burden of the White Christianized West is to save the world. As the distorting constructions of race and salvation overlapped, the mythology of White Jesus carried great social value for persons with approximate likeness in Europe and North America, social groups that became the new chosen people, replacing Israel.

Black Jesus

Theologian James Cone notes an astonishing historical fact: for over 50 years after the Civil War, White Christians participated in the lynching of almost 5,000 Black men and women but did not see the contradictory nature of their actions.[14] A verse from the book of Acts in the Bible says, "They put him to death by hanging him on a tree" (English Standard Version). This is in reference to Jesus, and the parallels between the violence that killed Jesus and the violence of White mobs that defended segregation, supremacy, and racial purity are both significant and eerily ironic. The practice of lynching and the method of execution on the cross, according to Cone, are "symbols of terror, instruments of torture and execution, reserved primarily for slaves, criminals, and insurrectionists—the lowest of the low in society."[15] The mythology of White Jesus, while imagined, has real social, psychic, civic, spiritual, epistemological, and ontological consequences that reinforce a racialized hierarchy of social power. In the 1920s, having endured centuries of religiously-sanctioned, White supremacist terrorism, violence, and systems of domination, Black Americans ushered in a movement of Black liberation and consciousness through a passionate renaissance of art, anthropology, literature, culture, philosophy, and spirituality in Harlem. Nathan Irvin Huggins, Harlem Renaissance scholar, observes,

> For it appears that in the decade of the 1920s, the Afro-American came of age. ... He proclaimed himself to be a man and deserving of respect, not a ward of society nor a creature to be helped, pitied, or explained away.[16]

For the "New Negro,"[17] White Jesus was an apparition of a system of White supremacy,

> To many African American Christians, pastors in Harlem, and intellectuals of the Harlem Renaissance movement, the white Christ was a problem. He represented a type of Christianity that served only to instigate black suffering. The God represented by the white Christ could be described as sadistic; he was a transcendent pedagogue who stood at a distance, coming near only to chastise the sinner with misery ... black Christians identify black suffering with Jesus' suffering.[18]

The image of a suffering Black Jesus inverted the structures of power represented in the iconography and mythology supporting White Jesus and signaled God's identification with the humanity, suffering, and liberation of Black people. God's wrath and judgment would deal with White supremacy. The ontological racism that the White architecture of salvation perpetuates is "an infection of self-loathing, spread by exposure to white racism that is carried as a parasite within modern colonial strains of a contaminated white Christian worldview."[19] The epidemic nature of White supremacy remains a catastrophic threat that reverberates in horrifying ways in the contemporary era.

The threat is demonstrated in egregious episodes of White supremacist violence, such as the 2015 Charleston church massacre in which an avowed White supremacist murdered nine Black worshippers in their Bible study at "Mother Emanuel," Emanuel African Methodist Episcopal Church. The disease of White supremacy must not be understood only as incidents like the recent march on August 11, 2017, where White protestors wielded torches in the night yelling, "You will not replace us," and "Jews will not replace us," around the Rotunda building and statue of Thomas Jefferson at the University of Virginia. The movement of White supremacists in the subsequent "Unite the Right" rally on Saturday, August 12, 2017, resulted in deadly violence that claimed the lives of three people and sent reverberations of shock across the country. President Donald Trump's interpretations of the incident sharply conform to the same racialized logic that led to his presidency. Beyond these incidents, White supremacy must be examined as a system.

While the engineers of the White architecture of salvation strive to buttress their claims of knowledge and power through the iconography of White Jesus, movements of prophetic imagination and resistance have also worked to dismantle systems of White supremacy and expand how human thriving is socially imagined. In the days of the Harlem Renaissance, for example, influential author and activist, Langston Hughes, penned a subversive poem, "Christ in Alabama," which reveals a countervailing trope that signifies Jesus *as* the oppressed. In a disruptive blow to White supremacy, Hughes exposes through Black prophetic imagination the logic undergirding it:

> Christ is a nigger,
> Beaten and black:
> Oh, bare your back!
>
> Mary is His mother:
> Mammy of the South.
> Silence your mouth.
>
> God is His father:
> White Master above
> Grant Him your love.
>
> Most holy bastard
> Of the bleeding mouth.
> Nigger Christ
> On the cross
> Of the South.[20]

Holding in mind the image Langston Hughes evocatively constructs, we recognize that "there is a relationship between Western articulated theologies and christologies and Western supremacist ideology which tends to perpetuate the oppression of the oppressed."[21] We maintain that the pandemic consequences of the White architecture of salvation demand the continuous and relentless pursuit of revolutionary change, and agree with bell hooks who writes, "all great movements for social change in our society have strongly emphasized a love ethic."[22]

We recognize "the idea of love as a transformative force,"[23] and strive to participate in the collective reimagining of what it means to live in freedom in ways that disrupt the interlocking systems of oppression.[24] When Cornel West writes, "Justice is what love looks like in public, just as deep democracy is what justice looks like in practice,"[25] we think about the role of social institutions, especially the unique positionality of colleges and universities, which are called to contribute to the public good. This book is principally concerned with the courageous and ongoing task of educational justice, which strives to dismantle systems of White supremacy and simultaneously imagine "deep democracy,"[26] particularly within the expansive and complex terrain of higher education. In doing so, the book has important implications for higher education research, policy, and practice.

Roadmap of the Book

The manifestations of White Jesus and the White architecture of salvation have historically emerged in a variety of settings. A strong defense of White dominance is through the normativity of White Jesus in White theological thinking. In 2017, when the Duke Divinity School sent a message to professors asking them to attend a diversity training, a full professor in a "reply all" email responded with another appeal:

> I exhort you not to attend this training. Don't lay waste your time by doing so. It'll be, I predict with confidence, intellectually flaccid: there'll be bromides, clichés, and amen-corner rah-rahs in plenty. When (if) it gets beyond that, its illiberal roots and totalitarian tendencies will show. Events of this sort are definitively anti-intellectual. (Re)trainings of intellectuals by bureaucrats and apparatchiks have a long and ignoble history; I hope you'll keep that history in mind as you think about this instance.
>
> We here at Duke Divinity have a mission. Such things as this training are at best a distraction from it and at worst inimical to it. Our mission is to thnk [sic], read, write, and teach about the triune Lord of Christian confession. This is a hard thing. Each of us should be tense with the effort of it, thrumming like a tautly triple-woven steel thread with the work of it, consumed by the fire of it, ever eager for more of it. We have neither time nor resources to waste. This training is a waste. Please, ignore it. Keep your eyes on the prize.[27]

In a simple email to Duke Divinity School faculty, the full professor reinforced an oppositional binary between diversity efforts and the mission to "teach about the triune Lord of Christian confession" as natural, which illustrates dominant White theological thinking. As people who work and teach in Christian higher education, teach diversity classes, and belong to Christian churches, we consider the work of valuing every tribe, tongue, and nation as central to our witnesses as followers of Jesus. We have outlined the following chapters to offer a roadmap of the book.

Essential to understanding the full breadth of how White theological dominance formed the symbolic image of White Jesus are biblical and historical pieces of the puzzle. When White European Christians fused White supremacy with divine doctrine as justification for the fifteenth-century European slave trade, the result was a theological reality of White ascendency and a religion embedded with Whiteness. Chapter 2, "White Civil Religion, Empire, and Dominance," explores the origins of how religion and empire became intertwined and how race and dominance came to play a role. Chapter 3 examines the ways in which Christianity became White and reviews its historical relationship with race, racism, and economic power in the U.S.—especially related to slavery, Jim Crow, and Civil Rights. Some of this chapter, as well as other sections of the book, appeared in earlier versions in Allison Ash's dissertation. Chapter 4 considers the contemporary movement of the Religious Right and how it more fully represents the "Religious White."

Chapter 5, "White Saviors and Proselytizing Pagans: Boarding Schools, Missionaries, and Adoption," begins a more topical lineup of arguments, beginning with a series of examples of conquest and expansion. Because this book is concerned with the intersection of race, religion, and education, Chapter 6, "White Christian University," explores the ways in which these dominantly White institutions have historically infused and continue to infuse White theology into the educational environment, which contributes to a religiously and intellectually laced version of White supremacy. Chapter 7, "White Worship," examines the ways in which worship styles illustrate the symbolic iconography that represents the structure of power. We pose questions that challenge current public policies, such as immigration, which are more American than biblical. Our premise is that Whiteness is so pervasive in America that most White Christian leaders cannot distinguish between what is White and what is Christian, and priority is often unwittingly granted to whiteness.

In Chapter 8, we offer thoughts about Jesus "before he became White," with biblical readings for justice. The chapter includes several key texts from the Bible to examine the role of following the first-century Jesus. These texts are an important way to conclude this volume, because White Jesus and the White architecture of salvation are outcomes of a diseased theological imagination, but integral aspects of the social construction of reality. If this reality has been socially constructed, it can be reconstructed with a better theology.

The Gospel invites the powerful to take up their cross and follow Jesus. Salvation for the powerful comes from the decision to give up power and take up the cross. … Because the powerless are already on the cross, salvation comes from endurance and faithfulness in the hope of God's deliverance through the resurrection.[28]

Lastly, in the Afterword, we will discuss the ongoing task of educational justice in light of our own limitations and shortcomings. We explore a very different image of Jesus that was painted in a mural in Los Angeles and almost immediately whitewashed. The concluding thoughts of the book include both lament, hope, and anticipation for justice and a clear vision of Jesus.

Notes

1. Cone, James H. *The cross and the lynching tree*. Maryknoll, NY: Orbis Books, 2011.
2. Corey, Barry H. "Contemplations on the Jesus Mural Decision," March 19, 2013. Retrieved from https://www.biola.edu/president/messages-media/contemplations-jesus-mural.
3. Mazza, Ed. "Racists Freak Out Over Black Santa at Mall of America," *Huffington Post*, last modified December 6, 2016. Retrieved from http://www.huffingtonpost.com/entry/black-santa-racists-freak-out_us_5844fb5ee4b09e21702f631b.
4. Gold, Hadas. "Megyn Kelly: Jesus and Santa Were White," *Politico*, last modified December 12, 2013. Retrieved from http://www.politico.com/blogs/media/2013/12/megyn-kelly-jesus-and-santa-were-white-179491.
5. Perkinson, James W. *White theology: Outing supremacy in modernity*. New York, NY: Palgrave Macmillan, 2004, p. 157.
6. Collins, Christopher S., and Alexander Jun. *White out: Understanding white privilege and dominance in the modern age*. New York, NY: Peter Lang, 2017.
7. Berger, Peter L., Thomas Luckmann, and Dariuš Zifonun. *The social construction of reality*. New York, NY: Random House, 2002.
8. Cone, James H. *God of the oppressed*. New York, NY: Orbis Books, 2008, p. 39.
9. Ibid.
10. Perkinson, 2004, p. 157.
11. Bailey, Sarah P. "White Evangelicals Voted Overwhelmingly for Donald Trump, Exit Polls Show," *The Washington Post*, last modified November 9, 2016. Retrieved from https://www.

washingtonpost.com/news/acts-of-faith/wp/2016/11/09/exit-polls-show-white-evangeli-cals-voted-overwhelmingly-for-donald-trump/?utm_term=.f1de9416b714.

12.   Shellnutt, Kate. "Trump Elected President, Thanks to 4 in 5 White Evangelicals," *Christi-anity Today*, last modified November 9, 2016. Retrieved from http://www.christianitytoday.com/gleanings/2016/november/trump-elected-president-thanks-to-4-in-5-white-evangel-icals.html.

13.   Williams, Reggie L. *Bonhoeffer's black Jesus: Harlem renaissance theology and an ethic of resis-tance.* Waco, TX: Baylor University Press, 2014, p. 41.

14.   Cone, 2011.

15.   Ibid., p. 31

16.   Huggins, Nathan I. *Voices from the Harlem renaissance.* New York, NY: Oxford University Press, 1995.

17.   Ibid.

18.   Williams, 2014, p. 25.

19.   Ibid., p. 81.

20.   "Christ in Alabama" from *The Collected Poems of Langston Hughes* by Langston Hughes, edited by Arnold Rampersad with David Roessel, Associate Editor, copyright © 1994 by the Estate of Langston Hughes. Used by permission of Alfred A. Knopf, an imprint of the Knopf Doubleday Publishing Group, a division of Penguin Random House LLC. All rights reserved. Any third party use of this material, outside of this publication, is prohibited. Interested parties must apply directly to Penguin Random House LLC for permission. The use of the n[word] is a struggle in writing about race. As a multiethnic group of authors, we considered the gravity of reprinting this poem and found that including it appropriately represented the iconic work and influence of Langston Hughes.

21.   Grant, Jacquelyn. *White women's Christ and black women's Jesus: Feminist Christology and womanist response.* Atlanta, GA: Scholars Press, 1989, p. 1.

22.   hooks, bell. *All about love: New visions.* New York, NY: William Morrow and Company, Inc., 2000, p. xix.

23.   Ibid., p. xix.

24.   Collins, Patricia Hill. *Black feminist thought: Knowledge, consciousness, and the politics of empowerment.* New York, NY: Routledge, 2009.

25.   West, Cornel, and David Ritz. *Brother West: Living and loving out loud, a memoir.* New York, NY: SmileyBooks, 2009, p. 232.

26.   Ibid.

27.   Dreher, R. "Duke Divinity Crisis: The Documents Are Out," *The American Conserva-tive*, last modified May 7, 2017. Retrieved from http://www.theamericanconservative.com/dreher/duke-divinity-crisis-griffiths-documents/.

28.   Law, Eric H. F. *The wolf shall dwell with the lamb: A spirituality for leadership in a multicultural community.* St. Louis, MO: Chalice Press, 1993, p. 42.

· 2 ·

WHITE CIVIL RELIGION, EMPIRE, AND DOMINANCE

This ideal of America is the hope of all mankind ... That hope still lights our way. And the light shines in the darkness. And the darkness will not overcome it.
— President George W. Bush, September 11, 2002[1]

In the beginning was the Word, and the Word was with God, and the Word was God ... In him was life, and that life was the light of all mankind. The light shines in the darkness, and the darkness has not overcome it.
— John 1:1, 4–5 (New International Version)

Introduction to Myths and Empire

Throughout churches in both wealthy suburbs and poor rural areas, people are filled with a zeal for Christ that interlopes with their zeal for country. The preceding quotes give credence to the ways in which a common "American" identity is messianic. The national myths of innocence, rightness, and White savior run deep in the identity of many American Christians—so much so that George W. Bush co-opted the message of John 1 and replaced the role of Jesus with the ideal of America. Artwork in Christian bookstores and clipart on church bulletins are rife with ways to overlay the flag on the cross and vice versa. The Holy Bible is one of the top three most sold and distributed books of all time. As a result, thematically-oriented versions of the Bible are popular ways to capitalize on sales. Consider, for example, the *American Patriot's Bible: The Word of God and the Shaping of America*, produced by Thomas Nelson publishers. This thematic Bible is marketed as:

> THE ONE BIBLE THAT SHOWS HOW 'A LIGHT FROM ABOVE' SHAPED OUR NATION. Never has a version of the Bible targeted the spiritual needs of those who love our country more than The American Patriot's Bible. This extremely unique Bible shows how the history of the United States connects the people and events of the Bible to our lives in a modern world. The story of the United States is wonderfully woven into the teachings of the Bible and includes a beautiful full-color family record section, memorable images from our nation's history and hundreds of enlightening articles which complement the New King James Version Bible text.[2]

The belief that America is a chosen nation is a deeply seeded myth that is expressed in art, images, rhetoric, and songs (e.g., *God Bless America*). However, this myth and architecture of salvation did not begin in the U.S.—the belief began much earlier. The image and ideology of a White Jesus is embedded in the development of empire and is expressed in civil religion, nationalism, and patriotism.

In early Christianity, followers of Jesus experienced an uncertain and contested relationship with the government. The Roman Empire periodically tortured Christians or disregarded them, which shaped how Christians thought about their citizenship. Sociologist Rodney Stark, nonetheless, credits the growth and proliferation of Christianity in its first three centuries to a variety of factors, including the rights it afforded to women and children, religious practices (e.g., helping the sick and dying during famine and epidemics), the willingness of its adherents to become martyrs in the face of tyrannical power, and the rule of fourth century emperor, Constantine, who sanctioned Christianity as the official religion of the Roman Empire.[3] To explore the relationship of religion and empire, this chapter examines Christianity's contemporary dominant social position in relationship to the U.S. Empire and discusses the prevailing civil religion that animates its dominance.

W. E. B. Du Bois captured the essence of how power and religious zeal came together to build supremacy, while also constructing inferiority:

> War, murder, slavery, extermination, and debauchery—this has again and again been the result of carrying civilization and the blessed gospel to the isles of the sea and the heathen without the law.[4]

The result is theologically justified conquest, a pattern that was noticeable in the treatment of Muslims throughout the crusades in Europe. Conflicting ideologies and xenophobic behaviors resulted in violent conflicts between Christian religious sects, ultimately leading to the reformation. Through church and state-sanctioned missions, legitimated Western knowledge and culture were spread, all the while classifying the receiving cultures as inferior. The *natives'* reception of this knowledge was not only a path to salvation, but civilization. The treatment of indigenous peoples, beginning with Columbus and reinforced through the notion of manifest destiny, was filled with epistemic and physical violence. Schooling systems, such as Indian Boarding Schools and in places like Hawai'i, served as central mechanisms through which native languages and practices were banned and eradicated (these examples are discussed further in Chapter 5).

Adding to the toxic combination of nation building and religious zeal, the continued belief in the establishment of a *Christian America* is key to perpetuating White Jesus and the White architecture of salvation. The belief that the *founding fathers* were evangelical Christians is a false premise often used to promote the crude idea that evangelical religious principles should be used to dominate the governance and existence of people today. The popular evangelical author and activist Tim LaHaye wrote, "Whenever I study the history of America, I am conscious that we are a miracle nation," which he further explained by writing that the purpose of the miracle was so that "God would establish one nation that would do more to fulfill His basic objective for this age, to 'preach the gospel to the ends of the earth,' than any other nation in history."[5]

The White architecture of salvation and the confluence of racism, conquest, belief, and power function together in ways that portray White Jesus as a normative and symbolic carrier of truth and meaning without the burden of justification. The dominant myth that the United States of America is a Christian nation is deeply ingrained and assumed. The origins and byproducts of this myth have been outlined in great detail.[6] Religious historian Richard Hughes illuminates the five religious myths that dominate U.S. society and are often invisible to their beneficiaries: the myth of the Chosen People, the myth of Nature's Nation, the myth of the Christian Nation, the myth of the Millennial Nation, and the myth of the Innocent Nation. Here, we extend the agenda Hughes established in the 2003 book, *Myths America Lives By*. In *Myths*, Hughes details the nation's most cherished myths, "stories that serve the nation in important and crucial ways," and regarding propagating national myths, writes, "we affirm the meaning of the United States."[7] In order to maintain their function, there are hidden and unconscious ways the myths work, for they "must remain invisible unless we name them, bring them to consciousness, and explore the way they have functioned—and continue to function—in American culture."[8]

Myths derive their power in that they are normative in the psyche of their benefactors, who rarely identify them or see the inherent contradictions. In outlining the mythologies, Hughes brings into dialogue "African American critiques" by highlighting Black freedom fighters like Harriet Tubman, Nat Turner, David Walker, and Frederick Douglass as witnesses to the myths' underside. We extend this methodology to critique U.S. wealth and power. We argue that the relationship between the state, racism, mythology, and civil religion forms a powerful constellation of forces that fuel the White architecture of salvation.

Merging Christianity and the State

In *Mere Discipleship*, Lee C. Camp sets out to reclaim notions of Christian discipleship. In doing so, Camp asserts that:

> If one's social location impacts or affects one's understanding of who God is and what God is concerned with, it would appear that the *church's* social location may affect its understanding of Jesus. For this reason, many have suggested that the meaning of "Jesus" depends on whether one finds oneself on this side of Emperor Constantine or the other.[9]

In considering the religion of the empire, Camp makes this crucial point: "Christianity becomes its own worst enemy: the 'triumph' of Christianity actually inhibits discipleship, for the masses already too easily believe themselves to be Christian."[10]

There are several unsubstantiated stories about emperors who led their armies to be baptized, all the while wielding their sword-bearing arms out of the water to demonstrate the violent collusion between empire and Christianity. Whether involving Charlemagne or Ivan the Great, stories of mass baptisms with a warmongering slant have never been reasonably proven. However, the historical record of the Emperor Constantine (born around 280 CE) is widely recognized as a point in Christianity when a turn toward empire and conquest occurred. The followers of Jesus were either disregarded or persecuted under the various rulers of the Roman empire. When Constantine was in a legendary battle outside of Rome in 312 CE, he had a vision of a cross made of swords in the sky. He then had his soldiers inscribe the letters Chi and Rho onto their shields. These are the first two letters of the word Christ in Greek.

The ensuing battle resulted in victory and Constantine was established as the new ruler of Rome. Constantine believed that God supplied the victory. During the almost quarter century reign of Constantine, Christians were afforded more freedom and less persecution than in the previous 300 years. Although seemingly a victory for freedom and religion, the nature of Christianity was altered by its relationship with the state. Constantine used Christianity to negotiate difficult issues of war, empire, control, and public relations. Four decades after Constantine died, Christianity was officially named the state religion, making it the only legal religion in the Roman Empire. At this moment in history, Christianity appears to have overtaken its enemies and established a Christian Kingdom—Christendom, the ultimate alliance between church and empire.

The establishment of Christendom ushered in centuries of political alliances and empires that were fueled with the belief that God sanctioned their violence. States acted with the authority of God and churches sanctioned the violence of states. In Europe, the division between Catholics and Protestants became part of state violence and crusades against other peoples. What was normalized in the Constantinian empire simply became reified in the violent conflict between Catholics and Protestants. The message of Jesus became heavily clouded by a long history of empire.

Race and Religion

Because race is fundamentally a social construct with social implications, it has evolved over time. There are a variety of arguments about when race as a social construction actually emerged. Some scholars have argued that race—and consequently, racism—did not exist in antiquity, although substantial evidence contradicts this claim.[11] A reason for this dismissal emerges from the use of modern-day concepts of race, namely phenotype, to interpret ancient racial classifications. However, while phenotype was an inherent indicator of group membership, it was not the primary way that societies racially classified their citizens. Ancient writings reveal proto-racism, the thoughts and ideas embedded in ancient Greco Roman culture that construe hierarchy and dominance.

When religion and human origins come together as an explanation for race, the categories become ontologically rooted—meaning that race signals something about the nature of being and the social hierarchy. The best example of this is the notion of the curse of Ham from the book of Genesis. Biblical passages that initially served to explain human origins were eventually misused and misinterpreted to justify the enslavement of Black peoples.[12] Genesis 9:20–27 recounts the story of Noah's sons, Shem, Ham, Japheth, who left the ark after the flood and saw their father naked after "he became drunk and lay uncovered inside his tent" (Genesis 9:21 New International Version). Ham reacted to his father's nakedness by telling his brothers. However, Shem and Japheth covered their father's naked body and left their father's tent without looking at him "so that they would not see their father naked" (Genesis 9:23). This interaction resulted in Noah praising Shem and Japheth but cursing Ham's son, Canaan, and proclaiming that Canaan would be enslaved to Shem and Japheth. Throughout the centuries, groups of people have interpreted Genesis 9:20–27 according to the social, cultural, and political needs of the time.

Origen, an early Christian church father, concluded that the Egyptians were Ham's descendants and cursed to slavery and servanthood. Origen described the color of the Egyptians, but he did not comment on skin color in association to Ham, nor did he connect skin color with servanthood as a prescribed reality. In the medieval era, one of the first Constantinople archbishops and a patristic theologian, Chrysostom (c. 349–407 CE), explained in a sermon that Ham sinfully lacked self-control resulting in his son Canaan being cursed, but he did not mention skin color.[13]

Race-based interpretations of this passage became evident only in the seventh century surrounding the enslavement of African peoples. When one group began using their power to dominate another people group, they began looking for ways to set themselves apart as distinct and superior. The dominant group highlighted physical distinctions to create this separation and resulting dominance, and interpretations of religious writings reflected the beginning of this cultural shift.

Beginning at the seventh century and onward, the reality of Canaan receiving the curse of servanthood (as opposed to Ham) began to disappear from biblical interpretations of Genesis 9. By the seventeenth century, Canaan was no longer in the theological equation and Ham was left as the biblical character to receive the curse. This interpretive shift meant that the incorrect etymology of Ham referring to "dark" or "black" had the opportunity to give rise to the connection between slavery and blackness. For example,

> The loss of Canaan enabled Noah's curse on Canaan to broaden into a Curse of Ham. The movement back a generation [from Canaan to Ham] allowed the curse to expand beyond just the Canaanites and thereby encompass all of Ham's children. The effects of this movement were devastating and the impact of that movement can still be felt in churches and society in general to this day.[14]

As a translation of Ham as "dark" or "black" solidified, the other characters in the story became identified as White European or Asian. With identification as the primary objective, people in positions of power could use the new interpretation for their socio-political needs. Put differently, Black bodies could be bought and sold using biblical interpretation as a justification. Therefore, the theory of Ham's descendants that eventually developed into the Curse of Ham provided a divine justification for the European and American slave trade, where White citizens legalized slavery in America in the seventeenth century with the Curse as a biblical justification.

Civil Religion

The introduction of this chapter includes a Bible that is a blend of patriotism and religion. A much older Bible that is approaching a 200-year anniversary is commonly referred to as the *Jefferson Bible*. In this ambitious project, the founding father, slaveholder, Virginian landowner, and former president Thomas Jefferson took up the task of literally cutting apart the Bible to create a revision of the Gospels that was consistent with human reason and enlightenment. It is called *The Life and Morals of Jesus of Nazareth*. Noticeably missing from the book are any miracles of Jesus, depictions of the adversary, and the resurrection of Jesus. According to the Smithsonian Edition of the *Jefferson Bible*, this bold project reflects much of the pervasive thinking regarding human reason of which Jefferson was a contemporary.[15] From our perspective, Jefferson's work is part of a long history of imperial distortions of Christianity to serve the state.

Although the term *civil religion* was first published by Rousseau in the eighteenth century, it was made popular in the 1960s in the U.S. by Robert

Bellah, who argued that civil religion is fundamentally different from Christianity. However, it can be difficult to distinguish the two concepts or beliefs when observing religious practice in the U.S. Civil religion is defined as the collection of beliefs, symbols, and rituals that shapes beliefs about society, which are exemplified in monuments, architecture, and experiences (i.e., movements). Through institutionalized collectivity, certain figures take on the status of prophet or savior (e.g., Jefferson and Lincoln), and texts like the Constitution take on the status of scripture. However, Bellah argues that this is not necessarily idolizing the state:

> Fortunately, since the American civil religion is not the worship of the American nation but an understanding of the American experience in the light of ultimate and universal reality, the reorganization entailed by such a new situation need not disrupt the American civil religion's continuity.[16]

Under Bellah's conception, civil religion can inspire a country to do great things with a sense of universal or general higher purpose. However, civil religion can also perpetuate a patriotism that can devolve into ethnocentrism and nationalism. Although the idea is to build inclusivity and universalism, the construction of a civil religion in the United States has been credited with piecing together a diverse nation, which occurred through settler colonialism, slavery, Jim Crow, and other racist and White supremacist policies.

Civil religion is in some ways a Faustian bargain (i.e., an exchange of morals or spirituality for some material gain). It may rally people to deeply feel the myths of exceptionalism, moral superiority, and rightness, and express those feelings through patriotic holidays and respect for the Constitution as though it were a timeless and God-given document. The use of religious and Christian imagery to infuse a sense of national superiority is dangerous for multiple reasons. The military conquests, xenophobia, and stratification within borders fall prey to religious justifications. Furthermore, even if civil religion was constructed as something universal, in the U.S. it borrows heavily from Christianity. And in another Faustian bargain, many Christians have taken the religiously infused language from the "Founding Fathers" to mean that the U.S. is a Christian nation.

The notion of a Christian nation does profound harm to the message of Jesus and to the freedom of choice or freedom from religion that should be open to all. As pictured in Figure 2.1, the enormous U.S. flag hanging on the basilica represents a merger of interests. It is no longer civil religion; it is patriotizing the message of Jesus, which in turn gives license to civil religion.

Figure 2.1: American Flag Draped on a Church.
Source: https://pixabay.com/en/basilica-washington-dc-religion-509724/.

Concluding Thoughts on "Giving to the Emperor"

Jesus entered into a social situation where the religious elite were complicit in working with Rome to advance the empire. When Jesus emerged as a leader, some of his followers thought he would lead an outright revolution against the empire. Jesus drew careful distinctions between rendering taxes and duties to the empire as opposed to faith and loyalty. The revolution occurred, however, not in the form of any previous revolution. The radical path of following Jesus called for being citizens of a different domain. An article in *Sojourners* describes the communion and tension in this way:

> Everyone is invited to join—there are no barriers, no borders, no walls—but citizenship comes at a cost. God's kingdom unavoidably confronts and challenges the many Caesars in our world, along with their supporters and their religious minions. They'll use Caesar's methods—bullying, harassment, intimidation, self-promotion, lying, verbal, and physical violence—to protect their privilege and power. The gospels tell

us that Rome and its religious minions conspired to try to get rid of Jesus and his advocacy for God's competing kingdom. The same thing happens today.[17]

The resistance to Jesus when he was alive persists through those who follow his message in a hierarchical and stratified world.

Consider when Jesus was asked an intentionally risky question about paying taxes (Luke 20). The question was risky because if he supported paying taxes to the emperor, then his loyalty to the Jewish faith would be questioned. Alternatively, if he supported the avoidance of paying fees to the imperial master, he might be in legal jeopardy. The political sensitivity of the question as to what faithful Jews should do was posed as a no-win situation—a trap. However, Jesus gave a response that was craftier than the question posed to him:

> "Show me a denarius. Whose head and whose title does it bear?" They said, "The emperor's." He said to them, "Then give to the emperor the things that are the emperor's, and to God the things that are God's."

People, made in the image and likeness of God, belong exclusively to God. His message is to pay taxes to the emperor but give the highest loyalty to God. Jesus refuses to support violent rebellion against Rome but is also not creating a sphere of life that is exempt from God's authority. Instead, a level of fidelity that supersedes any state obligation should be reserved for God. The inherently political nature of the trap set for Jesus corresponds to the inherently political distractions that may cause an imbalance of loyalty in terms of service and duty to God. For those who claim to follow Jesus, patriotism should never assume the fervor or make the absolute claims of religion. However, the lines are often blurred with laws, holidays, heroes, and the power of civil religion in times of international conflict. Nazi Germany was a test for Christianity and followers of Jesus. On the German side, soldiers wore belt buckles inscribed with the saying, "God with us." Karl Barth, a theologian, wrote the Barmen Declaration in an effort to confess the church's attempt to find a disposition in the world, which stood in opposition to the idea of adjusting its claims in service to an emperor.

Although there are Jesus-centered movements that have rejected imperialism, conquest, and an interloping with civil religion, the most dominant movements in Christianity have aligned with empire. Whether belief in the destiny of a revolution, the overtaking of a continent from one coast to the other, or the maintenance of oppressive and free labor, religious beliefs have to be reconciled with the viruses with which they have become infected.

Countermovements in Christianity (c.f., Anabaptists who were burned by Catholics and Protestants in Europe for being baptized as adults) may be criticized for being too separate from society and the state. However, they may also have much to offer those who claim to be Christians and may give some insight into how to disentangle the comingling of patriotism, empire, civil religion, and what Jesus intended for his followers.

Notes

1. Bush, George W. 2002. President's Remarks to the Nation. White House Archives. Retrieved February 20, 2018, from https://georgewbush-whitehouse.archives.gov/news/releases/2002/09/20020911-3.html
2. Richard Lee, Ed. *American patriot's bible: The word of God and the shaping of America*. Nashville, TX: Thomas Nelson, 2009.
3. Stark, Rodney. *The rise of Christianity: A sociologist reconsiders history*. Princeton, NJ: Princeton University Press, 1996.
4. Du Bois, William Edward Burghardt, and Brent Hayes Edwards. *The souls of black folk*. Oxford: Oxford University Press, 2008, p. 114.
5. LaHaye, Tim. *Faith of our founding fathers: A comprehensive study of America's Christian foundations*. Green Forest, AR: Master Books, 1994, p. 65.
6. Hughes, Richard T. *Myths America lives by*. Urbana, IL and Chicago, IL: University of Illinois Press, 2004.
7. Hughes details five myths: the myth of the Chosen People, the myth of Nature's Nation, the myth of the Christian nation, the myth of the Millennial Nation, and the myth of the Innocent Nation. Hughes, 2004, p. 2.
8. Ibid., p. 8.
9. Camp, Lee. *Mere discipleship: Radical Christianity in a rebellious world*. Grand Rapids, MI: Brazos Press, 2008. p. 21.
10. Ibid., pp. 22–23.
11. Buell, Denise Kimber. "Rethinking the Relevance of Race for Early Christian Self-definition." *Harvard Theological Review* 94(4): 449–476, 2001, Cambridge University Press.
12. Goldenberg, D. M. *The curse of Ham: Race and slavery in early Judaism, Christianity, and Islam*. Princeton, NJ: Princeton University Press, 2003.
13. Whitford, David M. *The curse of Ham in the early modern era: The Bible and the justifications for slavery*. Farnham: Ashgate Pub. Ltd., 2012.
14. Ibid., p. 104.
15. Jefferson, Thomas, Harry R. Rubenstein, Barbara Clark Smith, and Janice Stagnitto Ellis. *The Jefferson Bible: The life and morals of Jesus of Nazareth, extracted textually from the gospels in Greek, Latin, French & English*. Washington, DC: Smithsonian Books, 2011.
16. Bellah, Robert. "Civil Religion in America." *Dædalus* 96(1): 1–21, 1967, p. 18.
17. Kay, Joe. "Religion and Power were Intertwined. Then Jesus Challenged It All." *Sojourners*, November 27, 2017. Retrieved from https://sojo.net/articles/religion-and-power-were-intertwined-then-jesus-challenged-it-all.

· 3 ·

HOW CHRISTIANITY BECAME WHITE

Christianity for the Aryan is race—and race is Christianity
—White Supremacist Leader[1]

Introduction

Imagine that a White churchgoing Christian with conservative worship practices, social views, and beliefs about limiting the ability of women to participate in leading church, moves from the South to Southern California. Upon
arrival he may be quickly overwhelmed with traffic, the cost of living, and
how liberal many of the churches seem to be. Someone in this predicament
may report that many of these churches worship in spirit, but not in truth. In
Los Angeles, there are many congregations that adopt conservative worship
practices. Many of these congregations are predominantly Black or Korean
churches. For many White Christians, a White ethos outweighs any other
criteria for choosing a church.

In a 1960 interview on *Meet the Press*, Rev. Dr. Martin Luther King Jr.
offered his famous thoughts on Sunday morning church services representing
the most segregated hour in America:

I think it is one of the tragedies of our nation, one of the shameful tragedies, that eleven o'clock on Sunday morning is one of the most segregated hours, if not the most segregated hours, in Christian America. I definitely think the Christian church should be integrated, and any church that stands against integration and that has a segregated body is standing against the spirit and the teachings of Jesus Christ, and it fails to be a true witness. But this is something that the Church will have to do itself. I don't think church integration will come through legal processes. I might say that my church is not a segregating church. It's segregated but not segregating. It would welcome white members.[2]

King's analysis remains true. In this chapter we consider key moments and movements to explain how Christianity became White.

Christianity and Whiteness

There are intricate connections between Christianity and race, exemplified throughout history from antiquity to today by scholars[3] and Christian theologians.[4] Although the Christian faith centers around the personhood of Jesus—whose incarnational arrival was as a Middle Eastern man and whose message centered around the love of neighbor (Mark 12:31) and putting others' needs above one's own (Philippians 2:1–4)—Christianity as an institutionalized religion in the West has been a perpetrator of systemic racism by embedding an ideology of Whiteness into its structure. When Christianity became infused with the combined principles of power and Whiteness, the religion itself became a tool for dominance and oppression in the name of faith. Before modern constructions of race, fifteenth-century Christianity planted the seeds of White superiority in the heart of White Christianity through a racialized system of slavery in the name of Christianization. Those seeds were watered through features of society like an institution of slavery, scientific racism, and economies that reified White power. From the European Catholic Church to Evangelical Christians in America to Christian institutions of higher education, Whiteness has been a salient identity within Christianity for centuries.

By the time southerners began rebuilding their region following the Civil War—efforts known as Reconstruction—the stage had been set for racism to become the dominant force employed by White Christians to maintain the order of White superiority that slavery had inherently sustained for centuries. The stage where this rampant racism played out was the White response to Black progress during Reconstruction (1865–1877) and the resulting Jim Crow laws that legally segregated society between Black and White.

With the law of slavery no longer the formal keeper of White supremacy, the ideology had to evolve. A White architecture of salvation dictates an ideology of God-ordained inequity. Even though some White Christians were highly influential in the eventual abolition of slavery, the possibility of Black equality was nowhere to be found in the collective White imagination; they needed new shackles for White supremacy, namely, segregation along with the view of Black inferiority. As W. E. B. Du Bois stated, "The slave went free; stood a brief moment in the sun; then moved back again toward slavery."[5]

Reconstruction

Many Reconstruction efforts were initially successful for formerly enslaved Africans. In a few short years after the Civil War, African Americans filled 16 seats in Congress and 600 state legislatures.[6] The efforts of northern White Christians to assist in providing education and social services helped the southern Black community to begin integrating into White American culture and society, and for a brief moment in history formerly enslaved Africans and White people "rubbed shoulders … in a manner that differed significantly from Jim Crow of the future or slavery of the past."[7]

White Christians came to believe that the increasing involvement of Black citizens in American life threatened the ideal of the U.S. as a Christian nation because they did not believe that formerly enslaved Blacks had been evangelized or educated properly; leading evangelical leaders believed that America was meant to be a White society.[8] Southern White Christians had residual fears that "a literate slave was a potentially dangerous one,"[9] and both southern and northern Whites feared the prospect of Blacks becoming equals with Whites. The racial mindset of White Christians permeated U.S. culture in the nineteenth century, and as Black Americans began moving toward the prospect of racial equality the reaction intensified. In one particular instance in 1866, "White mobs in Memphis killed at least forty-eight Black people, gang-raped at least five Black women, and looted or destroyed $100,000 worth of Black-owned property."[10] Eventually in the South, Whites focused their efforts on creating Jim Crow laws used to maintain segregation.

Jim Crow Laws

Jim Crow laws carried "a system that was designed to isolate, subordinate, degrade—push down."[11] The little that is known about the origin of the term *Jim Crow* comes from a song and dance that Thomas Dartmouth Rice wrote in 1832 as a comedy called "Jim Crow:"

> Weel a-bout and turn a-bout
> And do just so.
> Every time I weel a-bout
> I jump Jim Crow.[12]

Although the reasons for using the name Jim Crow are unclear, Rice popularized the comic song and dance to the point where it was considered America's "first international song hit" in 1832, and by 1838, the term was "wedged into the language as a synonym for Negro ... a 'comic' way of life."[13] What began as a song and dance that mocked enslaved Africans evolved into a legal system that subjugated Black citizens for nearly a century.

Legal segregation and discrimination that started in the North preceded the formalized Jim Crow laws of the South. Even though slavery had been abolished almost completely in the North by 1830, northern Black people were subject to White supremacy. The lack of control through slavery meant that White people needed to find other means of control through laws and regulations. Well before the southern Jim Crow laws, Black citizens in the North were required to sit in designated spaces on buses, boats, and cars and did not even enter most restaurants unless they were servants.[14] In White churches, Black people would sit in segregated pews and had to wait for all of the White people to be served the sacrament of communion before they could partake.

Racial prejudice in the northern states persisted, in spite of abolished slavery. While White northern Christians have been lauded for their efforts in rebuilding the South after the Civil War, these Christians performed their service "with the conviction that they brought with them a superior culture and were sent by God to transform a fundamentally immoral society."[15] The North modeled for the South how to engage in post-slavery discrimination. The difference between the subordination during Reconstruction versus Jim Crow was that in the latter era, Black citizens were "totally segregated and needlessly humiliated by a thousand daily reminders of their subordination."[16] The separation of races included separate railroad cars, restaurants, saloons, and drinking fountains, bathrooms, and even a separate Bible over which witnesses would swear in a court of law.

Furthermore, Jim Crow made it legal to publicly beat, lynch, and hang Black people who were accused of breaking the law. It is estimated that between 1890 and 1917 "at least two to three black southerners were hanged, burned at the stake, or otherwise murdered every week."[17]

Segregation and the White Christian Mind

The prevailing mindset among White Christian leaders during this time period did not differ from White society at large. White Christians believed that society should be segregated, Black people should be second-class citizens, and that the White race was superior, leading White southern Christians to advocate for separation on both sides of the church doors. When members within the Presbyterian denomination suggested that Black people be given leadership opportunities in church government, the denomination as a whole advocated for separation. A racist belief circulated throughout churches was that God had created distinct races and therefore policies aimed at unifying the races were at odds with God's creation. Overall, southern and northern White Christians alike did not oppose Jim Crow laws and did not believe that these laws discriminated against Black citizens.

Other White Christians sought to reform some social injustices within society and began the social gospel movement. They founded the Federal Council of the Churches in Christ in America in 1908, but the council completely avoided or ignored the question of race.[18] Even though it existed for the betterment of society, for the first ten years of the council's existence it showed no action on addressing racial equality. Instead, its disposition and mission to Black citizens was to evangelize and educate. In fact, one of the leading figures of the social gospel movement, Josiah Strong, publicly expressed his White supremacist views in his book *The New Era or the Coming Kingdom*. He included an entire chapter titled "The Contribution Made by the Anglo-Saxon," in which he said, "they [the White race] exemplify a purer Christianity and are to-day a mightier power for righteousness on earth than any other race."[19] He went on to extol the White race and proclaim that no other race had been as philanthropic and moral as White people. He stated,

No race has ever shown such philanthropy, no race is so easily moved by great moral ideas, none is so capable of moral enthusiasm, none is so quick to accept responsibility for the ignorant, the degraded, the suffering, or to make generous self-sacrifice in their behalf as the Anglo-Saxon. … No doubt it [the White race] sacrifices more lives and more treasure for the uplifting of mankind than all other races combined.[20]

The obvious and great irony of this kind of comment is that Strong made these statements at a time when White Christians, almost entirely without consequence, were murdering Black citizens. Strong was proclaiming that, more than any other race, White people were enriching humanity, in spite of the fact that at the time White Christians were terrorizing Black citizens throughout the U.S. The murdering of innocent Black citizens was placed behind a guise of Christian benevolence, which is a different kind of enduring violence—the *violence of imagination* that believes that the White race will always be superior.

Jim Crow laws stayed in effect until the civil rights movement of the 1950s and 1960s. Before the racial progress of the civil rights movement, the U.S. faced some of the worst decades of White racial terrorism with White Christians at the center.

The Klan and the White Christian Norm

The Ku Klux Klan was an aggressive form of White supremacy that emerged near the end of Civil War and continues today as evidenced by the rallies at the University of Virginia and surrounding Charlottesville community. The Klan began as a group of White Christian terrorists localized in the South, but membership eventually spread into mainstream culture after the popularity of the first blockbuster film, *Birth of a Nation*, which represented a dominating White Christian mindset within the United States.

Originally founded by General Nathan Bedford Forrest of the former Confederate army in 1866, the Klan carried out "a reign of terror against freed people who refused to behave like slaves, against white Unionists, and against squatters of both races."[21] The fact that this group was historically considered a White *Christian* group[22] added to the horrors of its existence. During the Reconstruction era, the Klan's actions focused on maintaining White economic control of land by instilling fear and terror. The Klan's influence slowly waned until a resurgence in the 1920s when its impact moved beyond the traditional south and into states like Indiana, Oregon, and Colorado. Unlike the first wave of the Klan, this new surge of the 1920s Klan attracted members who were business owners, land owners, merchants, and community members who were all White, but occupied a variety of economic classes.

An instigation for the reawakening of Klan activities and membership was the 1915 release of D. W. Griffith's movie, *Birth of a Nation*. Based on the novel by Thomas Dixon, *The Clansman*, the movie caricaturizes the Reconstruction era as a time of "corrupt Black supremacists petrifying innocent Whites."[23] The movie's climax portrays a Black man hunting a White woman to rape her, which results in her dying by jumping off a cliff to escape. The story continues with the deceased woman's brother gathering Klan members to see that justice is done, and it ends with Jesus—a White Jesus—appearing to give his blessing on the Klan's victory. In theaters in the South, the movie "prompted whoops and wild cheers"[24] and "nearly 100 Blacks were actually lynched in 1915."[25] In one southern theater, film-goers became so engrossed in the movie that they used guns to shoot the screen.[26]

The film was fully embraced at the federal level, with President Woodrow Wilson screening a film for the first time at the White House. This presidential action gave moral sanction to the film and its message. Thomas Dixon, who had been Wilson's college roommate, used his connections to arrange the screening as well as showings for high-ranking legislators and even Supreme Court justices. Chief Justice Edward White quietly revealed to Dixon during the screening that he had been a Klan member himself.[27] The movie is considered to be Hollywood's initial feature-length movie, which gave rise to Hollywood and was the source of a nationwide motion picture industry with full distribution. Movie producers planned a robust marketing campaign to spread the White supremacist message of the film, including a billboard in Times Square portraying Klan members carrying burning crosses.[28] By 1916, millions of people had seen the film, making it the highest grossing movie in the United States for the next twenty years.

A "'Klan-mania' briefly swept the nation."[29] During this period of time, college students had Klan-themed costume parties. One could find Klan hats and aprons for purchase and advertisements to join the organization next to information about the film showings. As a result, Klan membership soared. It is estimated that from 1920 to 1925 membership rose from 2,000 members who were mainly from Alabama and Georgia to six million members from a variety of states from across the country. It was common to see Klan members in parades and carnivals and, at their public events, often up to 10,000 of members would gather, their appearances similar to descriptions of the zeitgeist in

Nazi Germany. During this time period, the Klan dominated communities and directed the individual lives of its members.

The film reflected the existing White racist mindset and also resulted in White supremacist racist ideas seeping further into U.S. culture due to the film's popularity and resulting Klan resurgence. The years following the release of Birth of a Nation were marked by racist violence; the summer four years later has been described as the "Red Summer" to represent "all the blood that spilled in the deadliest series of White invasions of Black neighborhoods since Reconstruction."[30] Even though the 1920s church press organizations were critical of the Klan, being White Protestant Christian was a prerequisite to become a member and many White Christian Protestant pastors were Klan members.[31] Put differently, not all people who identified as White Protestant Christians were Klan members, but all Klan members identified as a White Protestant Christians. Therefore, White Christianity served as a kind of sacred canopy covering the ethos and ideology of the organization. Birth of a Nation and Klan ideology are evidence that the mindset of the White Protestant Christian permeated American culture. When members of the Supreme Court and the President of the United States sanctioned the racist film, it legitimized racist hatred that spread throughout the country with the tacit stamp of approval from White Christians in seats of power. When this tragedy occurred, White Christian racism became solidified as a cultural phenomenon to the point that Klan members could wear white hoods in hometown parades and blend in with the accepted norms of Middle America culture.

Adding to the complexity of the Christian corroboration with White supremacy was the fact that even though six million White Protestant Christians, including pastors, were members of this organization, little evidence exists to demonstrate that churches offered overt allegiance to the Klan.[32] For many White Christians, espousing normativity and silence became the prevailing practices that fostered the enduring White dominant mindset. These practices continued into the time of the Civil Rights Movement when most White Christians remained silent in the fight for racial equality in the United States. The confluence of modern evangelicalism and politics in the decades that followed the Civil Rights Movement reified the union of Christianity and whiteness.

White Theology and the Complicity of Silence

White theologians and professors who serve as the architects and overseers for Christian higher education are overwhelmingly silent on issues of the

Christian church and its historical collusion with racism and White dominance. The historical realities presented in this chapter are rarely presented
in Christian higher education classrooms of Bible and theology. James Cone
lamented over this White silence of Christian theologians:

> What deepens my anger today is the appalling silence of white theologians on racism
> in the United States and the modern world. Whereas this silence has been partly
> broken in several secular disciplines, theology remains virtually mute. From Jonathan
> Edwards to Walter Rauschenbusch and Reinhold Niebuhr to the present, progressive
> white theologians, with few exceptions, write and teach as if they do not need to
> address the radical contradiction that racism creates for Christian theology. They
> do not write about slavery, colonialism, segregation, and the profound cultural links
> these horrible crimes created between white supremacy and Christianity. The cul-
> tural bond between European values and Christian beliefs is so deeply woven into
> the American psyche and thought process that their identification is assumed. White
> images and ideas dominate the religious life of Christians and the intellectual life of
> theologians, reinforcing the 'moral' right of white people to dominate people of color
> economically and politically. White supremacy is so widespread that it becomes a
> 'natural' way of viewing the world. We must ask therefore: Is racism so deeply embed-
> ded in Euro-American history and culture that it is impossible to do theology without
> being anti black?[33]

Cone referenced Jonathan Edwards as one of the silent White theologians
on matters of race. Edwards was silent on the issues of slavery and racism
because he himself owned slaves. Even in this century, White historians of
Christian higher education revere Edwards and his theological contributions,
specifically, regarding the idea that true virtue (as opposed to natural virtue) has
"its basis only in the saving grace of God."[34] According to Ringenberg, "Modern Christian academics especially ought to be able to learn valuable lessons
from Edwards as they plan their own strategies for effective use of learning."[35]
For some, Edwards' theological prowess may appear too great for Christian
higher education leaders to neglect even though he did not speak out against
the evil institution of slavery and, in fact, actively participated in it. However,
there should be an honest excavation of how influential figures like Edwards
contribute to the White architecture of salvation through the reality of his
past and his complicity in the kind of silence. Edwards continues to be considered one of the most significant contributors to the theology upon which
Christian higher education stands. However, educators must bring to light
today that even with Edwards' critical theological contributions, his theology
was severely lacking when he remained silent on a theology of the oppressed
and enslaved. Cone spoke to the contradiction of modern White theologians

extolling Edwards for his fight against moral philosophy but remaining silent on the fact that Edwards was colluding with the system of slavery,

> Christianity was blatantly used to justify slavery, colonialism, and segregation for nearly five hundred years. Yet this great contradiction is consistently neglected by the same white male theologians who would never ignore the problem that critical reason poses for faith in a secular world. They still do theology as if white supremacy created no serious problem for Christian belief. Their silence on race is so conspicuous that I sometimes wonder why they are not greatly embarrassed by it.[36]

In a 2012 lecture at a leading Christian higher education institution, an African American pastor shared his thoughts about Edwards' theological contributions versus his practice of slave ownership, "It is a dangerous dichotomy to separate the man from his theology … his socio-cultural construct and his theology might not push him to worship with me, but it ought to keep him from owning me."[37]

The White Christian theologians and leaders who served as establishing members of Christian churches, denominations, societies, and colleges in the United States created a foundation for the proliferation of an indoctrination guided by a Christian worldview and Christian ideals. Many of these U.S. institutions that were formed in the eighteenth, nineteenth, and early twentieth centuries are flourishing with steady membership and enrollment and producing leaders who are committed to Christian service and the betterment of society. A stain of White supremacy marked this movement from its beginning. From schools and churches intentionally prohibiting attendance and admission to Black parishioners and students, to holding overtly discriminatory policies, to remaining primarily silent on their Christian White supremacist past, Christian institutions have a deep legacy of racial injustice that has not been adequately addressed.

Conclusion

An ideology of White superiority perpetuated White Christians to participate in, and often lead the way in, some of the most racist, oppressive, and abhorrent beliefs and practices in modern history such as scientific racism, eugenics, the Transatlantic Slave Trade, White terrorism, and Jim Crow laws. Even White Christians who led the way to end slavery held views of White racial superiority. Through the practice of inaction and voicelessness, White churches have perpetuated racism and White dominance in Christianity. Our concern is not just historical and a quest for acknowledgement. The roots of the White architecture of salvation are still intact. Not only do the branches of this movement need to be pruned, but the roots need to be rehabilitated to reverse the Whitewashing of Jesus and the radical movement of followers of Jesus.

Notes

1. Toy, Eckard. "'Promised Land' or Armageddon? History, Survivalists, and the Aryan Nations in the Pacific Northwest." *Montana: The Magazine of Western History* 36(3): 82, Summer 1986.
2. King, Martin Luther. April 17, 1960. *Meet the Press*. Retrieved from https://www.youtube.com/watch?v=1q881g1L_d8
3. Kendi, Ibram X. *Stamped from the beginning: The definitive history of racist ideas in America*. New York, NY: Nation Books, 2016.
4. Sechrest, Love L. *A former Jew: Paul and the dialectices of race*. New York, NY: T&T Clark International, 2009.
5. Du Bois, W. E. B. *Black reconstruction: An essay toward a history of the part which black folk played in the attempt to reconstruct democracy in America, 1860–1880*. Original Work published in 1935. New York, NY: Russell & Russell, 1976.
6. Ngai, Mae M. "Race and Ethnicity in America: A Concise History." In *Race, nation, and citizenship in late nineteenth-century America, 1878–1900*, edited by R. H. Bayor. New York, NY: Columbia University Press, 2003, pp. 96–130.
7. Woodward, C. Vann. *The strange career of Jim Crow*. New York, NY: Oxford University Press, 2002, p. 26.
8. Emerson, Michael O, and Christian Smith. *Divided by faith: Evangelical religion and the problem of race in America*. New York, NY: Oxford University Press, 2000.
9. Reimers, David M. *White Protestantism and the Negro*. New York, NY: Oxford University Press, 1965, p. 22.
10. Kendi, 2016, p. 240.
11. Bennett, Lerone J. *Before the Mayflower: A history of black America*. 5th ed. New York, NY: Penguin Books, 1984, p. 257.
12. Ibid., p. 255.
13. Ibid., p. 256.
14. Woodward, 2002.
15. Doyle, G. Wright. *Christianity in America: Triumph and tragedy*. Eugene, OR: Wipf and Stock, 2013, p. 150
16. Woodward, 2002, p. 44.
17. Ngai, 2003, p. 103.
18. Reimers, 1965.
19. Strong, J. "The New Ear or the Coming Kingdom." Retrieved from https://web-a-ebscohost-com.ezproxy.wheaton.edu/ehost/detail/detail?vid=1&sid=0543249f-6b56-419a-a208-74c1b748f385%40sessionmgr4010&bdata=JnNpdGU9ZWhvc3QtbGl2ZQ%3d%3d#anchor=GoToAllQVI&A, 1893, p. 55.

20. Ibid., p. 56.
21. Evans, William McKee. *Open wound: The long view of race in America*. Urbana, IL: University of Illinois Press, 2009.
22. Miller, Robert Moats. "A Note on the Relationship between the Protestant Churches and the Revived Ku Klux Klan." *The Journal of Southern History* 22(3): 355–368, 1956.
23. Kendi, 2016, p. 306.
24. McVeigh, Rory. "Structural incentives for conservative mobilization: Power devaluation and the rise of the Ku Klux Klan, 1915–1925." *Social Forces* 77(4): 1461–1496, 1999, p. 1464. doi:10.2307/3005883.
25. Kendi, 2016, p. 306.
26. Evans, 2009.
27. Ibid.
28. McVeigh, 1999.
29. Ibid., p. 1464.
30. Kendi, 2016, p. 314.
31. Miller, 1956.
32. Ibid.
33. Cone, James. *Risks of faith: The emergence of a black theology of liberation, 1968–1998*. Boston, MA: Beacon Press, 1999, pp. 130–131.
34. Ringenberg, William C. *The Christian college: A history of Protestant higher education in America*. 2nd ed. Grand Rapids, MI: Renewed Minds, 2006, p. 20.
35. Ibid., p. 26.
36. Cone, 1999, p. 131.
37. Dates, C. "Lecture Presented at Trinity International University at the Conference, Jonathan Edwards and American Racism: Can the Theology of a Slave Owner be Trusted by Descendants of Slaves?" *Lecture presented at Trinity International University*. Retrieved from https://www.youtube.com/watch?v, 2012, January.

· 4 ·

THE RELIGIOUS WHITE

Too narrow a front in battling for a moral crusade, or for a truly biblical involvement
of politics, could be disastrous. It could lead to the election of a moron who holds the
right view of abortion.[1]

—*Christianity Today*, 1980

Introduction

An ideology of White Evangelical Christianity became embedded in the
U.S. through the spiritualization and mass acceptance of political agendas
formed to accrue and maintain White systemic power. Although these ideas
were not biblically based, religious tradition and text were manipulated to
justify their widespread adoption within the White evangelical community in
America. At its very inception, White Evangelical Christianity was exclusive
and oppressive in nature, and these threads are still part of the fabric of White
evangelicalism today. This fabric is characterized by an inability to distinguish
politics from faith. Upon further examination of the history of and trends
within White Evangelical Christianity, it is clear that cultural and civic influences on beliefs and behaviors are ultimately attributed to God and biblical
commandments. Power and dominance that are constructed as God's desire

become an abuse and appropriation of God in the image of dominant peoples, movements, and powers. In that way, the son of God was made to be White. One product of American civil religion is a combination of *Christian* values and *White* values—an evolving conflation of cultures that occurred through several generations in American society.

The contemporary White Jesus is a current manifestation of White Evangelical Christianity, which is a distortion of the biblical Jesus, who disrupted, agitated, fulfilled prophecy, and was crucified for all of this. Historians have documented how some White Christians committed horrible racial atrocities in the name of God, while a vast majority of others remained silent in their complicity, and allowed racism to persist with impunity, while an unpopular minority of Christians partnered in the fight against racial injustices and were labeled liberals. The purpose of this chapter is to excavate superiority as a component of the White architecture of salvation, even among the people who were attempting to make positive change. As significant laws were passed to prohibit unjust systems such as slavery and segregation, those laws did not change the minds and narratives of the religious right, or the *religious White*. The syncretism embedded in White Evangelical Christianity has fundamental shortcomings that are manifested both in politics and the church. There are roughly 600 years of unfinished business to be addressed in the culture of White supremacy and hegemony in the U.S. People of color in Christian communities have, by and large, been fighting the battles of justice while the White community has been complicit through silence, ambivalence, and inaction.

Christian institutions have had a long and complex history of racial oppression or a profound absence from working for justice in society. Christianity in the U.S. has embraced power and aligned with political ideology. For example, the bold pro-life position is typically combined with silence around children living in poverty, and the death penalty is typically combined with state-sanctioned violence against men and women at the hands of law enforcement. The pro-life position is woefully limited but has built a platform on seeking changes in national legislation and celebrating celebrities like White Christian Tim Tebow for taking up the cause. At the same time, the kneeling of Black Christian Colin Kaepernick in protest to state-sanctioned violence against Black people was condemned as divisive. Beyond these high-profile topics, conversations in White evangelical churches have become centered on the question of whether Christians ought to use the term White privilege, as it has been associated with secularism. Sometimes those who bemoan an overly politically correct movement and its language policing then pivot and dictate which words should not be used by Christians. Perhaps it is part of human nature to attribute negative meaning to certain terms in order to justify the removal of words that generate feelings of discomfort.

Why would White Christians resist the idea of White privilege? Perhaps it is rooted in a misunderstanding of merit. Some resist the notion because it opposes the notion of meritocracy, achievement, hard work, and ultimately the protestant work ethic—the idea that God's blessings are apparent in people who work hard and have jobs, provisions, and wealth. The problem relates back to a paradox within the Christian church about whether one is saved by faith or effort. A fundamental idea within evangelical Christianity is that an individual cannot earn salvation but can only be saved by grace and faith alone. For example, in response to the Trump administration ban on Muslims during the refugee crisis, conservative White evangelical pastor and author David Platt posed the challenge, "Let's not respond to the refugee crisis from a worldview that's more American than biblical."[2] This challenge is not just about refugees—it addresses a deeper and more fundamental mindset for the American Christian because it interrupts the seamless thinking of American civil religion.

Systematic theologian Wayne Grudem used his evangelical celebrity as a platform to endorse then-presidential candidate Donald Trump as a values-based candidate who would be good leader to maintain a Christian nation. Shortly after the 2016 presidential election, evangelist Franklin Graham added, "I believe that God's hand intervened Tuesday night to stop the godless, atheistic progressive agenda from taking control of our country."[3] Other White evangelical Christian leaders such as "Focus on the Family" founder James Dobson often write or speak on behalf of all Christians by claiming that there is a homogenous Christian way of conducting oneself. In this context, however, the Christian way is a proxy for a politically conservative and dominantly White way in America.

At a convocation service at Liberty University, President Jerry Falwell Jr. made comments in response to the December 2, 2015, mass shooting in San Bernardino, CA. He advocated for students to carry guns on campus and stated, "I've always thought that if more good people had concealed-carry permits, then we could end those Muslims before they walked in ... and killed them."[4] An evangelical leader encouraged the preemptive killing of Muslims. However, several student groups wrote back to him to protest—an important part of the story about a campus that is homogeneous and dominantly White.

A critical examination is necessary to deconstruct the White architecture of the Christian mind that led to the election of President Donald
Trump. Jesus of Nazareth was born into a political system where the powerful
oppressed others for the sake of their own benefit. Jesus purposefully entered
this system, but his interaction with the politics of his time was not hoarding
power, but a surrendering it—even unto death. The person of Jesus was killed
by a dominating political system while he was attempting to challenge its
oppressing force. This picture of Jesus is a stark contrast to the White Jesus
who guides many White evangelical Christians to attain and maintain power
for personal and group self-interests today. The idea of the White evangelical
Christian is particularly important to examine in this chapter because of the
way in which the political meaning has come to supersede the theological.
Tracking this evolution is essential in order to comprehend evangelical attitudes toward race and politics.

Consider Billy Graham, who became successful with his large-scale
evangelistic crusades and experienced the tension of being separated from
American culture yet attempting to reach the culture at the same time. In
response to this tension, he became part of a larger effort of many fundamentalist Protestants who were working to become political insiders again.[5]
Graham maintained that his most salient motive was Christian conversion
and to oppose the growing tide of Protestant liberalism while simultaneously
forging friendships with political leaders to the point that he "became a
regular visitor to the White House through many administrations."[6] When
Graham passed away in 2018 at the age of 99, his body lay in honor at
the United States Capitol for a day of remembrance. He is only the fourth
private citizen in American history to lie in honor at the United States
Capitol.

Graham's interactions with political liberals created a break between
fundamentalist Christian leaders such as Bob Jones and Jerry Falwell, who
opposed any association with liberalism and the "larger group of conservative Protestants, who still held to the traditional fundamentals of the faith,
but were trying to reenter or stay in the mainstream."[7] The latter group
espoused an ideology of cultural engagement rather than the separatism
of the fundamentalists[8] and became known as "neo-evangelicals" or simply "evangelicals."[9] Even with the increased focus on cultural engagement,
evangelicals continued to espouse an ideology of individualism fueled by
theological, sociological, and democratic ideals. It is this ideology that has
been a driving force in perpetuating the White Christian mindset to today.

The Politics of White Individualism

Martin Luther made the argument that "Each individual … was accountable for her or his spiritual well-being to God through Jesus."[10] Individual salvation has been a primary doctrine of evangelicalism from its beginnings. "Freewill individualism,"[11] a view that White evangelicals have historically embraced, is the idea that people can create their own destinies, meaning that individuals are responsible for their own outcomes in life. Consequently, White evangelicals tend to think that equal opportunities for success or failure exist for all people, which directly impacts their political attitudes and behaviors. This also corresponds with an American ideology of democracy that emphasizes personal liberty and freedom. The combination of the doctrine of personal salvation, freewill individualism, and the context of the American democracy has created resistance to engaging in matters regarding racial justice and equity, and a political attitude of disregarding race.

White evangelicals have answered problems of racial injustice with a focus on individuals rather than racist systems. Put differently, a White evangelical mindset includes the belief that individual racist attitudes can be changed through Christian conversion and urging Christian kindness to achieve equality and racial justice. White evangelical Christians "opposed personal prejudice and discrimination, but not the radicalized social system itself,"[12] which would have required political intervention for lasting change. For example, Billy Graham believed that "the answer to the race problem was Christian conversion and love"[13] and that "organized reform efforts [for racial equality] were likely to do more harm than good."[14]

This White individualistic mindset played perfectly into the scheme of segregation. Although L. Nelson Bell, who was the editor of the *Southern Presbyterian Journal*, publicly supported desegregation in the 1950s, he believed that individual freedom—the right to segregate if one desired—superseded any action "by the government or by the church hierarchy" to formally desegregate society. For Bell, "[the] issue was freedom in the sense of individual rights."[15] In other words, he used his position to critique political intervention for the purposes of racial justice and maintained that politics were meant to protect individual—not group—freedom. J. Howard Pew, a financial contributor to the Christian publication *Christianity Today* and a Texas oil businessman, spoke in March 1958 at the National Council of United Presbyterian Men. He stated that a fundamental aspect of Presbyterianism was individual freedom and that the church should "not meddle in government affairs."[16]

White evangelical leaders continue to espouse the tenets of individualism, evidenced by leaders such as the prominent White evangelical pastor John Piper, who posited that the individual sins and "failings of the human heart that Jesus changes by the power of his gospel are the root causes of racial and ethnic disharmony."[17] White evangelicals tend to respond to problems of racism from an individual mindset (i.e., *but I don't own slaves*) and understand racism to be only overt and malicious racial acts (e.g., the Klan, skinheads) rather than complicity and silence. It is this individualism that has caused White evangelical Christians to demand political separation with regard to racial justice, but political integration with matters of individual freedom. White evangelical Christians remaining politically silent on issues of racism is a component of the individualistic mentality and serves as the modern-day example of the politically White disposition.

The Politics of White Silence

Political silence on issues of racism and the ideology of White normativity has permeated White Christian spheres, even in the face of immense racial injustice. Between 1957 and 1965, critical years of the Civil Rights Movement, *Christianity Today* published "less than two articles per year on race issues"[18] despite the reality that racial justice and equality were at stake at the time. Even as arguably one of the most well-known and most successful Christian evangelists of modern times, Billy Graham succumbed to White normativity when he wavered back and forth between conducting segregated and desegregated crusades depending on what was customary at a given crusade location. After being criticized by segregationists for his openness to racial integration at one of his crusades, he said,

> I feel that I have been misinterpreted on racial segregation. We follow the existing social customs in whatever part of the country in which we minister. As far as I have been able to find in my study of the Bible, it has nothing to say about segregation or nonsegregation. I came to Jackson to preach only the Bible and not to enter into local issues.[19]

Even though Billy Graham eventually forbade segregation at his meetings following the *Brown v. Board of Education* decision, he never "could accept the methodology of Martin Luther King and the Civil Rights movement."[20]

Although the passing of Civil Rights laws and the concept of political correctness has assuaged some of the overt forms of racism such as legalized segregation and legal forms of brutality, many of those issues have been replaced with modern forms of Jim Crow and lynching such as mass incarceration[21] and police brutality. U.S. prisons represent a new kind of slavery and the police officer's gun has been used as a new lynching rope. And instead of White preachers in the South using the Bible to defend their views of Black inferiority and clergymen citing authors who championed the ideology of scientific racism to publicly argue for White superiority, there is a lot of political silence about race from White evangelicals. Silence perpetuates a spirit of White complicity. Some White people attend Black Lives Matter rallies and may comment on social media outlets when they see videos of police officers killing unarmed Black citizens. However, very few White evangelical organizations—churches or otherwise—speak and act with unified political voices and hands to combat racial injustices today. With today's White evangelicals, silence is overt. Silence regarding matters of race is not, however, the same as political silence. In fact, White evangelical Christians have been some of the most coveted voters in modern U.S. history precisely because of their political engagement. The complex relationship between the demand for a moral vote and the supply of Christian thinking in politics has become a chicken-and-egg sort of issue. Put differently, it was not White evangelical Christians inserting themselves into the political milieu that created this distinct voting demographic. Rather, it was the political milieu that inserted itself onto White evangelical Christians, resulting in the extreme conservative political racial separatists that became known as the Religious Right.

Politics of the Religious White

White evangelicals have consistently claimed that political disposition is intricately connected with moral values and is therefore a tool for maintaining Christian morality in society.[22] The hypocrisy between doctrine and the actual practice of White Christians during the era of slavery is, in retrospect, unmistakably discernable. However, the hypocrisy that accompanies the White evangelical Christian in relation to a commitment to voting for morals and the tenets of the Christian faith did not disappear after the abolition of slavery, the Reconstruction era, Jim Crow laws, or even the civil rights movement. This hypocrisy set the stage for the creation of the White evangelical voter as a distinct demographic beginning in the 1970s and its strengthening during the Ronald Reagan era of the 1980s.

In the 1970s and 1980s, the connection between evangelicalism and politics strengthened to a fulcrum when *Newsweek* magazine named 1976 "The Year of the Evangelical"[23] in reference to the presidential election of that year. The biggest political shift, however, occurred in 1980 when conservative evangelicals such as Pat Robertson, who had passionately supported Jimmy Carter for president in the 1976 election, shifted their political allegiance to Ronald Reagan. During the Carter administration, a "politically and religiously conservative" organization had "coalesced as a political movement,"[24] which became known as the Religious Right. This group needed a political platform to support Bob Jones University, which had been denied tax exemption status in 1975 for forbidding interracial dating (a policy that did not change until 2000), and they looked to the issue of abortion to elicit political support from conservative Christians.[25] Therefore, racial separatism was at the inception of the Religious Right movement, but it was masked by the moral issue of abortion.

Even though Jimmy Carter self-identified as an evangelical Christian, Ronald Reagan represented a candidate who more closely aligned with the politically conservative ideals of the Religious Right. The hypocrisy of the Religious Right's support of Reagan centered around a misalignment with two key areas that were of interest among White evangelicals during the 1980 election: pro-family and pro-life. Reagan had assisted in the legalization of abortion by signing a bill when he was governor of California, and he had been divorced. Leaders of the Religious Right celebrated Reagan's victory and "heralded Reagan's election as a harbinger of the Second Coming." According to Balmer, "Reagan's election in 1980 and his reelection four years later cemented the political alliance between the Religious Right and the Republican Party."[26]

Regarding matters of racial justice, the solidification of the White evangelical with the Republican Party is notably problematic. This fusion has separated two primary political issues that White evangelicals claim are biblically imperative (abortion and gay marriage) from other Christian values (e.g., racial justice) that are important to consider in political discourse and decision-making. The quote at the beginning of this chapter is from a *Christianity Today* article titled "Getting God's Kingdom Into Politics." This article was written in 1980, when the political tide began to shift to this two-issue ticket for White evangelicals. The article was meant to assist Christians in clarifying their views on important political issues. Although the writer supported pro-family and pro-life views, the writer also offered a warning for Christians who might decide their vote based solely on the issue of abortion:

The concerns of the religious lobbies will appeal to a broader range of Christians to the extent that they emphasize these other equally biblical principles of justice, peace, stewardship of our resources, and care for the poor, as well as pro-family and prolife issues. It is a case of "these ye ought to do but not to leave the others undone." Too narrow a front in battling for a moral crusade, or for a truly biblical involvement of politics, could be disastrous. It could lead to the election of a moron who holds the right view of abortion.[27]

The final sentence of this quote appears prophetic given the 2016 election in which President Donald Trump received 81% of the White evangelical vote.[28] Many White evangelicals reported voting for Trump begrudgingly; however, they cited Trump's position on abortion as their voting rationale.[29] Although Donald Trump had joked about sexually assaulting women,[30] stated publicly that forgiveness is not something that he seeks from God,[31] had been alleged to have caused small business owners to declare bankruptcy as a result of not paying them for their work to build the Trump Organization,[32] and had been divorced twice at the time of the 2016 election, White evangelical Christians demonstrated with their vote where their priorities fall.

Political loyalty for the majority of White evangelical Christians now appears to have little connection with religious morality. Prior to the 2016 election, only a minority (30%) of White evangelicals believed that a politician could behave ethically in their political duties if they behaved personally immoral. However, in 2016, that number jumped to 72%. In other words, by 2016, the majority of White evangelical Christians no longer believed that personal morality is an important contributing factor to a politician's ethical behavior.[33]

Based on overwhelming support for Donald Trump in 2016, it is also clear that White evangelicals placed no political emphasis on racial justice because Trump's overt racist views did not dissuade White evangelical voters. His history of overt racism includes discriminating against Black renters (and being sued for such in 1973);[34] insisting for years that President Obama's birth certificate was a fraud; arguing that, although DNA evidence proved their innocence, five Black and Latino teenagers should receive the death penalty after being accused of rape against a White woman; and publically naming immigrants from Mexico as rapists, to name only a few.[35]

The statistics demonstrating morality losing importance in White evangelicals' voting patterns and their overwhelming support of an overtly racist president demonstrate the way that political loyalty—or White self-interest—has been engrafted into the minds of White evangelicals. A major shift has

been occurring from the 1980 to the 2016 elections that has solidified Whiteness, politics, and power as the center of White evangelicalism in the United
States. The majority of today's White evangelical voters are more concerned
about maintaining political power than preserving religious morality or plac-
ing biblical ideals at the center of their politics. The warning that *Christianity
Today* offered at the beginning of this religious/political engrafting in 1980
became a reality. The Religious Right is in many ways synonymous with the
Religious White.

Political Packaging and Marking

Political packaging occurs when institutional leaders bundle otherwise disparate issues into a monolithic category that connects a conviction to a political
ideology, regardless of whether the person holding that conviction identifies
with the stated political ideology. The result of political packaging is essen-
tializing a person into "conservative" or "liberal" based on a particular conviction that has become politicized without knowledge of the person's actual
political viewpoints. Political packaging only occurs, however, after an issue
had become politically marked.

 Political marking is the process by which anti-racism advocacy becomes
politicized. Once this issue becomes politically "marked," it is then bundled
along with the rest of the issues associated with that political position. So, for
example, because racial justice often becomes politically marked as liberal in
Christian higher education institutions, the people who engage in racial justice or speak out about racial justice issues are politically packaged with all of
the other issues associated with a liberal agenda. Therefore, political marking
and political packaging work together; when a person embraces a concern
that has been politically marked, that person is then politically packaged.

 A significant problem with political marking and packaging is that they
can cause leaders of Christian institutions (churches, colleges, etc.) to avoid
addressing issues of injustice because of a fear of being associated with the
political issues of the party to which the injustice has been connected, or
worse, being labeled as one with heretical views. Political packaging works
effectively to reduce engagement from others with disparate beliefs. When
White theologians and leaders couple racial justice movements with an ideology like neo-Marxism and, thus, label them as unbiblical, any individuals
associated with racial justice work will intentionally or unintentionally be

linked to unbiblical practices. For example, if addressing White privilege has been marked as a politically liberal agenda, those who attempt to educate others about White privilege may become identified as individuals who support the political pro-choice movement, a position on abortion that has been traditionally associated with a politically liberal party. The result is a distancing from issues associated with that political agenda, a solidification between the institutions and the Religious White, and an emphasis on maintaining a particular political agenda rather than fulfilling the institutional mission. One president of a Christian higher education institution addressed this issue of politicizing justice and criticized evangelicals for their lack of engagement in issues that have become politically marked. About such issues, he said, "If I preached about them, many people would get uncomfortable (no matter what I said), and a lot of people would begin to wonder if I've become a crazy liberal, or perhaps a crazy conservative."[36]

Attempting to remain connected to the political agenda that institutional leaders perceive as the *correct one* is often related to maintaining control and financial stability that political power may afford. We have witnessed university leaders convey an allergy to discussions of social justice and White privilege as a mirror to what happens in conservative politics. The terms are called divisive and counter to Christian ideals. It is very difficult for churchgoers, students, staff members, and professors to disentangle the political ideologies from morality and faith. While church leaders are pointing to the fear of a liberal agenda invading church-related institutions with a political agenda of liberalism, an overwhelming majority of White evangelicals continue to align their vote with conservative politics. This connection to a particular political party has become paramount to other moral and biblical issues of our time.

Conclusion

The invisibility of the White architecture of salvation and its existence in American evangelicalism has led to a strong attachment to power. The unchecked and unchallenged motivations for power, fed by misguided faith and false imagery of a White Jesus, have crept into politics, and this has led to many unhealthy representations of Christianity in the United States. As authors, we have been forced to interrogate our own preconceived notions of political correctness and the *natural* affiliations that seem to emerge from certain types of social activism. We intend for our efforts at self-interrogation to help expose unholy unions between politics and religion and the ways in which systemic associations influence individuals. Furthermore, we are also wary of actions and dispositions that convey solidarity with the oppressed and at the same time consciously accumulating power. The social, political, and religious movements that culminated in the Religious White are buttressed by a vision of a White Jesus and are at risk when compared to the biblical record of the actions, attitudes, and radical ideas of Jesus.

Notes

1. "Getting God's Kingdom into Politics," *Christianity Today* 24(10): 10–11, 1980. Retrieved from https://0-search-proquest-com.patris.apu.edu/docview/200671750?accountid=8459
2. Platt, David. "How to Respond to the Refugee Crisis," *The Gospel Coalition*, January, 2017.
3. Chapman, Michael W. "Rev. Graham: God Intervened Nov. 8 to Stop 'Atheistic, Progressive Agenda' in America." Cybercast News Service CNSNews, November, 2016.
4. Baily, Sarah Pulliam. "Jerry Falwell Jr.: 'If More Good People had Concealed-carry Permits, then We Could End Those' Islamist Terrorists," *Washington Post*, December 5, 2015. Retrieved from https://www.washingtonpost.com/news/acts-of-faith/wp/2015/12/05/liberty-university-president-if-more-good-people-had-concealed-guns-we-could-end-those-muslims/?utm_term=.0c4e7d88cdf4.
5. Ibid.
6. Ibid.
7. Marsden, G. M. *Religion and American culture.* San Diego, CA: Harcourt Brace Jovanovish Publishers, 1990, pp. 217–218.
8. Balmer, R. *Thy kingdom come: How the religious right distorts faith and threatens America.* New York, NY: Basic Books, 2006, p. xiii.
9. Marsden, 1990, p. 218.
10. Balmer, 2006, p. xiii.
11. Emerson, Michael O., and Christian Smith. *Divided by faith: Evangelical religion and the problem of race in America.* New York, NY: Oxford University Press, 2000, p. 98.
12. Ibid., p. 46.
13. Ibid., p. 47.
14. Ibid., p. 46.
15. Chappell, David L. *A stone of hope: Prophetic religion and the death of Jim Crow.* Chapel Hill, NC: The University of North Carolina Press, 2004, p. 117.
16. Ibid., p. 139.
17. Piper, John. *Bloodlines: Race, cross and the Christian.* Wheaton, IL: Crossway, 2011, p. 227.
18. Emerson and Smith, 2000, p. 46.
19. Martin, William. *A prophet with honor: The Billy Graham story.* New York, NY: William Morrow and Company, Inc., 1991, p. 170.
20. Emerson and Smith, 2000, p. 47.

21. Alexander, Michelle. *The new Jim Crow: Mass incarceration in the age of colorblindness*. Rev. ed. New York, NY: The New Press, 2012.
22. Hynes, Patrick. *In defense of the religious right: Why conservative Christians are the lifeblood of the republican party and why that terrifies the democrats*. Nashville, TN: Nelson Current, 2006.
23. Balmer, 2006, p. xvii.
24. Ibid., p. xvi.
25. Ibid.
26. Ibid., p. xvii.
27. "Getting God's Kingdom into Politics."
28. Goldberg, Michelle. "Donald Trump, the Religious Right's Trojan Horse," *New York Times*, January 27, 2017. Retrieved from https://www.nytimes.com/2017/01/27/opinion/sunday/donald-trump-the-religious-rights-trojan-horse.html.
29. McLaughlin, Seth. "Pro-life Voter Will Begrudgingly Support Trump," *The Washington Times*, October 31, 2016. Retrieved from http://www.washingtontimes.com/news/2016/oct/31/donlad-trump-gets-pro-life-voters-support-begrudgi/.
30. Goldberg, 2017.
31. Scott, Eugene. "Trump Believes in God, but Hasn't Sought Forgiveness," *CNN Politics*, July 18, 2015. Retrieved from http://www.cnn.com/2015/07/18/politics/trump-has-never-sought-forgiveness/index.html.
32. Reilly, Steve. "USA TODAY Exclusive: Hundreds Allege Donald Trump Doesn't Pay His Bills," *USA TODAY*, June 9, 2016. Retrieved from https://www.usatoday.com/story/news/politics/elections/2016/06/09/donald-trump-unpaid-bills-republican-president-laswuits/85297274/.
33. Kurtzleben, Danielle. "POLL: White Evangelicals Have Warmed to Politicians Who Commit 'Immoral' Acts." *NPR*, October 23, 2016. Retrieved from https://www.npr.org/2016/10/23/498890836/poll-white-evangelicals-have-warmed-to-politicians-who-commit-immoral-acts.
34. Kristof, Nicholas. "Is Donald Trump a Racist?" *New York Times*, July 23, 2016. Retrieved from https://www.nytimes.com/2016/07/24/opinion/sunday/is-donald-trump-a-racist.html.
35. Leonhardt, David, and Ian Prasad Philbrick. "Donald Trump's Racism: The Definitive List," *New York Times*, January 15, 2018. Retrieved from https://www.nytimes.com/interactive/2018/01/15/opinion/leonhardt-trump-racist.html.
36. Wytsma, Ken. *The myth of equality: Uncovering the roots of injustice and privilege*. Downers Grove, IL: InterVarsity Press, 2017, p. 94.

· 5 ·

WHITE SAVIORS
PROSELYTIZING "PAGANS"

Missionaries, Boarding Schools, and Adoption

Take up the White Man's burden—
Send forth the best ye breed—
Go bind your sons to exile
To serve your captives' need;
To wait in heavy harness,
On fluttered folk and wild—
Your new-caught, sullen peoples,
Half-devil and half-child.

—Rudyard Kipling, 1899[1]

Introduction

One principal characteristic of Christianity is rooted in the idea of expansion. Often called *The Great Commission*, Christians have seen the task of proliferating the message of the Bible throughout the world "in all Judea and Samaria, and to the ends of the earth" (Acts 1:8 NIV) as essential. In the New Testament, followers of Jesus go to great lengths to establish more churches and convert more people to the movement and belief in Christianity. The tradition continued, as noted in a previous chapter, with different levels of intensity when Christianity became a state religion under

Constantine. The notion of evangelizing a message of hope and "spreading at all cost" eventually experienced a strange shift from the sacrificial cost being placed upon the messenger (that oftentimes led to martyrdom), to a cost upon the recipient, which has led to various forms of coercion, torture, and death. Consider the crusades and inquisitions in Europe, imperialism around the world, and the application of manifest destiny in the U.S. These conquests and pursuits occurred with a sense of religious zeal. In this chapter, we interrogate the White architecture of salvation through discussing the White Savior mindset and the by-products as evidenced in boarding schools, uncritical missionary work, and transracial adoption. Although they may be seen as a stain on the history of Christianity, it is important to understand how passion for sharing a message can go awry. How did the Christian faith, which began with a Middle Eastern Jewish carpenter, become an institutionalized form of White dominance and power?

The 1872 painting *American Progress* by John Gast presents a spiritual and flowing image of a more-than-human woman drifting West. In front of her, indigenous people are fleeing; in her wake, trains, farmers, and White settlers follow. It appears as though she is carrying a holy text, perhaps the Bible, but upon close examination, it says "SCHOOL BOOK." Here, a single image projects the intersection of race, religion, and education. The pursuit of curing "pagans" of their "barbaric" ways in the name of progress has given conquest a religious zeal that has manifested in many movements and forms throughout history.

With each movement in Christian religious history, the idea of spreading truth became more paramount and took on different strategies and characteristics. From grassroots movements to gaining state-sanctioned power and dominance, the means of spreading White dominant Christian culture, thought, and practice continue to evolve. In this chapter, we interrogate the potentially destructive and devastating consequences to society when White Jesus is employed as a mechanism of White supremacist social control. As a final note, we also think about the message of Jesus as one that is profoundly worth spreading, but how it must be cleansed from the violent, oppressive, and aggressive ways it has been fashioned. In thinking about redeeming the complex notion of spreading ideas, we look to movements that embody (instead of misappropriate) the humility of Jesus in the first century.

To understand further the White architecture of salvation through the image and concept of a White Jesus, this chapter explores proselytizing those who are considered "pagans"—that is, people who hold a belief other than

Figure 5.1: *American Progress* by John Gast.
Source: Prints and Photographs Division, Library of Congress[2].

Christianity. With no intent to be comprehensive, three distinct examples are presented in this chapter: missionaries to Hawai'i, Indian boarding schools, and the complexity of adopting children. Each of these examples provide powerful insights into the ways in which White architectures distort and bleach our understanding of Jesus, who represents mercy and justice as opposed to dominance and conquest.

Missionaries in Hawai'i

Oh, honest Americans, as Christians hear me for my downtrodden people! Their form of government is as dear to them as yours is precious to you. Quite as warmly as you love your country, so they love theirs ... The people to whom your fathers told of the living God, and taught to call "Father," and whom the sons now seek to despoil and destroy, are crying aloud to Him in their time of trouble; and He will keep His promise, and will listen to the voices of His Hawaiian children lamenting for their homes.[3]

—Queen Lili'uokalani, 1898

The preceding quote is from the last queen of the sovereign nation of Hawai'i, before powerful sugar planters and the U.S. military engaged in an illegal takeover of the islands in 1893. Her plea was not heard, in spite of her faith, and the events that led to the takeover were rooted in the arrival of visitors to the islands. Early missionaries in Hawai'i bonded with the indigenous peoples and showed respect for their culture by assisting in making Hawaiian a written language. A wave of second-generation missionary activity served efforts to ban Hawaiian language, dancing hula, and other cultural practices. In this second wave, missionaries exploited the educational system to transmit White dominant Christian religion, and in turn, used religious thought in efforts to erase Hawaiian culture. Similar to the perceptions of indigenous peoples, the White architecture of salvation and concomitant White Savior mindset generated ontological perspectives on the existence of Native peoples that denied any value to their way of life, knowledges, beliefs, and practices.

In the early 1800s, a man named Henry Obookiah lived in New England and attended several academies.[4] His parents were killed on the Island of Hawai'i and he worked as a sailor, which allowed him to board a ship that traveled all the way to New York. There, he was adopted by a family of missionaries which led him to become a missionary himself and return to his home islands. Although he died in 1818 and was unable to complete that mission, he is known as the seed leading to the first missionary ship that arrived to plant in Hawai'i in 1820. Although it took them almost half of a year, the New England missionaries took the voyage from Boston to a land of "pagan" darkness, to build schools and churches. Upon arrival, one Reverend wrote of the "barbarism … almost naked savages" which led some of their group to cry and turn away while others in their group asked, "Can these be human beings?"[5]

Less than two years later, the missionaries had settled in and been welcomed into community. They played a role in evolving the Hawaiian language from oral only to written, with the advent of a seventeen-letter alphabet (later reduced to 13 including the okina). In 1839, the first Hawaiian-language Bible was complete and evangelists preached in Hawaiian and people of status were converted to Christianity. This first wave of missionaries represents some preservation of knowledge, some respect for culture, and even clear ownership of the Christian faith by Native peoples. However, even though this first wave showed some positive signs, the missionaries could not resist the power of the White architecture of salvation and worked to ban hula dancing. Hawaiian nobles who converted to Christianity promoted the ban and eventually regulated hula events with a fee system. The first ban occurred in 1830 and by 1857 the Hawaiian Evangelical Association began to actively seek a legal ban on hula.[6]

Alongside the idea of banning hula, the Sugarcane industry grew and the Royal School, where many children of the Hawaiian royal families attended school, was founded. The schools lifted the literacy rate in Hawai'i to one of the highest in the world and, as the economy grew, missionaries merged with the merchant class. At this point, the Protestant work ethic (equating hard work with being godly) became a sign of personal salvation, making this utilitarian theology a key marker of the White architecture of salvation. Hula was cited in a petition written by missionaries to the House of Representatives as a sin that caused people to be lazy and not work. In 1859, it was officially banned. During the same time, the children of early missionaries became powerful and wealthy landowners through sugar exports, and schools either deemphasized or banned the Hawaiian language.

In an effort to turn the tide of Westernization, Queen Lili'uokalani, a Christian who directed her church choir, took note of how cultural conflicts, disease, and disproportionate wealth were killing her people. When she became Queen in 1891, her effort to change the constitution to restore the monarchy led to an illegal takeover of Hawai'i in 1893, when a group of sugar planters and businessmen grew nervous and used their power to enact a coup. They also enlisted the help of the U.S. military. The Queen openly committed to not engaging in a violent clash to prevent the loss of life. The Queen was imprisoned and the annexation of Hawai'i was justified as a natural consequence of historical evolution. Only three years later, in 1896, the use of Hawaiian language in public and private schools was outlawed, and a series of policies contributed to *epistemicide* (mass destruction and murder of knowledge),[7] which was ultimately prevented by a renaissance of Hawaiian language and culture in the 1970s.

Similar to the destruction of indigenous peoples in the U.S., the small islands of Hawai'i suffered from colonial capitalism and religious moral arguments from the Hawaiian Evangelical Association, which worked in concert with colonizers to control and influence education, religion, policy, and politics. All of this culminated in military action to take over a sovereign nation. The White architecture of salvation is clearly demonstrated in the elevation of Christian values over traditional practices at the hands of the missionary establishment—even when indigenous peoples and leaders had fully adopted Christianity. In this episode of Jesus distorted by Whiteness, capital interests became the value system, or master, by which the planters and mercantilists engaged force to protect their investments.

Indian Boarding Schools in the Continental United States

A great general has said that the only good Indian is a dead one, and that high sanction of his destruction has been an enormous factor in promoting Indian massacres. In a sense, I agree with the sentiment, but only in this: that all the Indian there is in the race should be dead. Kill the Indian in him and save the man.

—R. H. Pratt, 1892[8]

In Indian civilization, I am Baptist, because I believe in immersing the Indians in our civilization, and when we get them under holding them there until they are thoroughly soaked.

—R. H. Pratt, 1883[9]

Richard Henry Pratt was an army officer who founded the Carlisle Indian Industrial School in 1879. It was the model for federal boarding schools designed to replace indigenous cultures, languages, and religion with something more civilized. Based on Pratt's record, the preceding quotes, and various addresses and publications, he had a very specific approach to religion, education, and conquest. His philosophy and outlook were distinct and clear, and in his autobiography, *Battlefield and Classroom*, Pratt said the goal for education of an "Indian" is "complete civilization" and his "absorption into our national life," which meant that "the sooner the Indian loses all his Indian ways, even his language, the better it will be for him and for the government."[10]

Pratt had been trained in the military and came up through the ranks as an officer who had many interactions with Native peoples in various forms. His purpose in being placed at such a formative location was, in fact, to help the "Indians." The numerous writings and addresses by Pratt and the extensive number of children educated under the system instituted by Pratt demonstrate the intersection of religion, education, and White supremacy. It also demonstrates how U.S. policy emerged from genocide to *epistemicide* for the 36,000 Native students who attended Carlisle or institutions like it by 1889.[11] The conquest to colonize and Christianize Natives from the inside out was aggressive and pervasive. Pratt fashioned the schools based on military practices and used various means to document the transformation of the students—most notably photography. Images of students in traditional Native dress placed next to the same student in an English suit and tie were used as publicity pieces in newspapers and elsewhere. Pratt's intense initiative was distinctly violent to tribal cultures and values, all the while being done in the name of being a benefactor.

It is easy to demonize the work of Pratt and others, who, under the guise of helping, made directly disparaging comments about Natives and used that as a means to generate policies and programs to eradicate their way of life. In addition to the individual personalities at the center of that history are collections of White Christian philanthropists and liberals who created a group called "Friends of the Indian." They believed in the incorporation and assimilation of "Indians" as a progressive measure. The Board of Indian Commissioners in 1880 added that,

> As we must have him [Indians] among us, self-interest, humanity and Christianity require that we should accept the situation and go resolutely to work to make him a safe and useful factor in our body politic. As a savage we cannot tolerate him any more than as a half-civilized parasite, wanderer or vagabond. The only alternative left is to fit him by education for civilized life.[12]

The confluence of an objective view of progress and dominance on one hand, and religious fervor under the sacred canopy of a White Jesus on the other, led to a deeply held belief system that savages are actually stuck in an earlier stage of social evolution. Lewis Henry Morgan, a pioneer in the field of anthropology, demonstrated the ways in which the White architecture of the mind converged with the White architecture of salvation through codified stages of social evolution. Native tribes were placed in early stages called *savagery*, with only a few placed in a higher stage called *barbarism*. Some of the markers of people reaching the highest stage of *civilization* include: Christianity, industrial advancement, and property ownership.[13] Adding this element of social science to the religious justifications led the progressive "Friends of the Indian" to play an important role in working to integrate the *savages*.

Education, even with Christian roots, can serve to mold people to serve dominant social interests. In the Carlisle school, children spent half of the day in religious settings like the chapel or classroom and spent half of the day learning industrial training, which simply meant manual labor. Schools modeled after Carlisle continued to be run by military leaders through the 1930s. Students wore military-style uniforms and stood and marched in lines in an attempt to cultivate civilized behaviors, Western linear concepts of time, and Christian respect for work. In these federal institutions, Christianity was man-datory. The Protestant work ethic and White dominance had given way to another wave of Christian conquest.

The Browning Ruling in 1896 declared that parents had no right to designate the school where their child would be enrolled. Practices of extracting children from reservations to place them in boarding schools became common, and the ongoing impact of the schools included accidents on work sites, loss of language and culture, profound homesickness, and dis-ease.[14] There is much more that has been and should be said about the ways in which multiple forms of power collide to create realities where people and knowledge are assimilated or annihilated. In brief, Indian Boarding schools are a profound example of how salvation and education are constructed to discipline the world into civilization by White Saviors in the name and image of a White Jesus.

The interactions and indoctrinations of Native children via education also spread into the aggressive practice of adoption. In some cases, chil-dren were forcibly removed from families to go to boarding schools, and in other cases they were placed in the care of other families. It was not until 1978 when the Indian Child Welfare Act was passed that tribes were give more legal authority. Colonial schooling then transformed into familial colonization:

> Transracial and transnational adoption is a reproductive justice, disability justice, racial justice, and decolonization issue. Transracial adoptees live with the lifelong impact of cultural erasure, exploitation and tokenism, cultural and linguistic theft, and abandonment and familial trauma. Transracial adoption has been used as a tool of cultural genocide, especially for indigenous and First Nations children stolen from their families and tribes and nations. Transracial and transnational adoption has also often been a tool of white proselytization through Christian "civilizing" missions meant to rescue children of color from our own cultures and societies so we might be "saved" by white, Christian families.[15]

An ethic in Christianity is to identify what is broken in a person or in society. White dominant Christianity identified anything non-white and non-European as vile, savage, and barbaric, thus profoundly fashioning new Christians by violence and force under the image of a White Jesus. The next section moves from education to focus further on the complex topic of adoption.

White Families and Brown Children

Marginalized bodies are constantly silenced and rendered invisible not simply through the failure to take issues of race and social oppression seriously but through the constant negation of multiple lived experiences and alternative knowledges.[16]

Thinking of adoption transracially? Make sure you buy all the essential items for your child. Set your child up for life? The must have items are …
1. One healthy dose of self-hatred
2. Two spoonfuls of gratitude
3. A cupful of desire to look just like you …
4. A lifetime of racism
5. A ricochet of resilience.[17]

The preceding quotes are from books that compiled poetry and other creative reflections from people who experienced transracial adoption. Children are vulnerable. Children without parents are at risk. Millions of children around the world are institutionalized, and some families feel an internal motivation to become the parents of orphaned children. There is no doubt that disenfranchised youth are in need of assistance. However, adoption is complicated. Moreover, transracial adoption adds a deeper level of complexity to an already complex relationship. The final section of this chapter is a departure from the previous two examples, but it is included with great intention. As overt acts of imperialism and colonization are less frequent, the advent of economic and epistemic colonialism is still prevalent. Similarly, as efforts from missionaries are not often linked to state power any more, some religious efforts are still manifested at the expense of cultures and traditions that may not actually be at odds with Christianity at all—just at odds with the White architecture of salvation. In this section, adoption is explored as a potential tool to alleviate some of the impacts of losing parents upon vulnerable children, and we examine the potentially negative impacts of familial colonialism. Whereas the preceding two sections highlight the collusion of capitalism, conquest, and Christianity, this section focuses on how moral and religious intentions to care for children can actually perpetuate psychological hardships and epistemicide in the black and brown bodies that are adopted by White families.

The 2018 Winter Olympic games were held in Pyeongchang, South Korea. Much of the news beyond the sporting events centered around the unified representation of athletes from North and South Korea. Although this was not the first time that athletes from the two divided nations marched in together, this was the first time that South Korea had granted permission for Korean-American adoptees to compete for South Korea. This inclusion led to a handful of media-driven human interest stories about ethnic Korean American athletes who chose to compete for South Korea, in search of both an Olympic medal and their birth parents. This change in policy, and the decision of Korean American adoptee athletes to compete for Korea, certainly brought greater national awareness of transracial adoptee stories. Many babies and young children born in Korea were orphaned and later adopted by White American families in the United States. A large proportion of adoptive families were Christians living in the Midwest. Many White families have been encouraged to adopt through global adoption organizations like Holt International.

Inspired by a film about biracial White-Asian (Amerasian) children in Korean orphanages and by Christian principles, Harry and Bertha Holt were an American couple who adopted eight Korean children and later founded an adoption agency in 1956. Thousands of White American families have worked with Holt International to adopt transracially, even to this day. It is worth noting the particular date and timing of the Holt agency's founding. The war in Korea, which began in June 1950, did not end with the signing of an armistice in 1953 that divided the Korean nation in half and separated families for the next seventy-plus years. With a fratricidal war among Koreans, why were there so many Amerasian babies? According to some reports,[18] tens of thousands of biracial babies came to the U.S. via Korean mothers and the American soldiers who fathered them. Stories of orphaned mixed-race children continue to unfold, but what is never clear is whether these Amerasian babies were conceived out of love, prostitution, or rape. During the Cold War era in the 1950s, good Christian men desiring to serve God and country came to the defense of a "poor nation" about to be lost to socialism and left broken and full of mixed-race children who would ultimately be cared for by other well-intentioned White American families.

In early conversations with a woman I (Collins) was dating, we quickly realized that we each had an independent desire to adopt. For her, the memory point of origin was a documentary on Romanian orphanages she watched as a child. For me, there was no single starting point, but a desire to adopt that grew as I got older. From the time we committed to marry each other, we knew we would include adoption as part of our family plan—which involved a compelling spiritual motivation connected to our Christian faith. Although the decision to adopt was easy for us (and our "plan A" for building a family), the actual process was difficult, time-consuming, emotional, and expensive.

Our interest in international adoption required us to make decisions about country of origin, age, sex, and ability and then go through numerous trainings, investigations of our personal lives, and payments of what seemed to be an enormous amount of money for us. This cost felt strange. During the adoption process, we were challenged to understand our desire to adopt. Ethiopia appeared to have the greatest need and important protections for children, so we chose to place our application there and started the process of waiting. We were exposed to criticisms of adoption—especially transracial adoption—which forced us to ask about the function and purpose of adoption and the heartbreaking number of institutionalized children in the world. Externally, friends and family asked us many questions like, "Why does it take so long? Why is it so expensive? If there are kids in need, shouldn't they be placed with willing families?" The tension grew in us as we sat between the critique of adoption from some corners of our world and the confusion about why it was taking so long from others.

During the international adoption process, a friend called and asked if we were willing to have a baby (to be born in six weeks) placed in our family. We said yes and our lives changed forever. Many years later, the international adoption process came to fruition—not in Ethiopia, but in China. I am White, Kristy is Mexican and White, our son Mateo is Mexican, and our daughter Adela Bao Yu is Chinese. We are easy to spot in a crowd.

Because adoption is a theological concept found in the Christian Bible and something that is often seen as part of the Christian narrative, it is an important part of the White Jesus construct. In this chapter, my (Collins) personal story is centered, but the fundamental purpose is to highlight the ways in which White and Christian families combine their faith, identity, and desire to love a child to create transracial families with black and brown children. When cultural identity and race get Whitewashed in Christian love, children may have all of their physical needs met, but may suffer emotionally and spiritually for a lifetime. A colorblind attitude with a mantra of "love is enough," can create a disjuncture between how children are raised in White homes and how they experience a dominantly White world.

When Kristy and I were in Guangzhou, China with dozens of other families meeting their children, we noticed that almost all of the families in our hotel and at the consulate were White. We estimated that during our two weeks there we encountered more than eighty families. The conflicted feelings grew as we saw White women and men carrying Chinese children with severe disabilities, Down syndrome, missing limbs and digits, enlarged craniums, and a variety of other challenges. Race and ethnicity were not often discussed by the families at the last stage of this process, but they were at the forefront of my mind and I remember saying to myself, "Surely these children will benefit even from well-meaning colorblind, White families." I think I even reflected on this aloud at breakfast one day and someone asked if I had read *Adopted for Life*, by Russell Moore. I responded no and he suggested that I read it because, in his words, "it pretty much goes against a lot of the training we had to do for transracial, international adoption."

Upon returning home, I ordered the book immediately and found the conflict embedded in the plentiful theological descriptions of adoption. Moore describes the process of adopting two Russian boys and of becoming a family. Although his children were adopted many years ago, he describes the adoption process as including the encouragement to teach children about their birth culture. Moore recognizes that the counsel was to include Russian folk tales, songs, and holidays, and writes:

> But as we see it, that's not their heritage anymore, and we hardly want to signal to them that they are strangers and aliens, even welcome ones, in our home. We teach them about their heritage, yes, but their heritage as Mississippians ... They learn about their people before them in the Confederate army and the civil rights movement. Yes, I'll read Dostoyevsky and Tolstoy to them one day, I suppose, but not with the same intensity with which I'll read to them William Faulkner and Eudora Welty ... They are Moores now, with all that entails.[19]

In the following paragraphs, Moore backtracks to say they are not trying to "obliterate" the Russian identity of the two boys and gives examples of talking to people from Russia about the town where the boys were born. This white-on-white type of epistemicide is yet another complex version of White Saviorism.

In another passage, Moore talks about renaming the boys and wrote: "There came a day when one could cry out 'Maxim' or 'Sergei,' and no one would respond [their new names are Benjamin and Timothy]. Those old names now meant nothing to them."[20] He acknowledges the resistance some people gave them to renaming the children and even quotes one book that advises against renaming because it can "interfere with the continuity of the child's life" or "interfere with their sense of self."[21] Moore disagrees, and the justification for disagreement is religious in nature as he explains that if there were fewer White, Black, blue-collar, and white-collar churches, it would allow people to see Jesus in a new light with one Spirit, one Father, and one Christ. A spirituality of colorblindness is the answer.

Continuing this line of thinking, Moore conflates a bigoted approach to adoption with liberal social workers and adoption experts who offer insights on complications with transracial adoption. Simply put, if a bigot says you should not adopt a brown child and a social worker cautions against transracial adoption, what is the difference? He also claims there are no studies that have proven any kind of psychological harm or social harm for children in transracial and adoptive families. Moore cites the claim that adoptive "children often face major challenges as the only person of color in an all-white environment, trying to cope with being different," as having no real foundation.[22] Along this line of thinking, Moore adds, "I'm not surprised to see secular social workers or sociologists suggest that racial identity could be more important than familial love … The gospel, though, drives us away from that kind of identity in the flesh and toward a new identity."[23] These sentences succinctly summarize the White architecture of salvation under the shadow of a White Jesus. We do not see a culturally responsive appreciation of birth culture and race as negating an identity in Christ, whereas Moore's reductive approach links the two.

Adoption is an ever-evolving phenomenon, and the critiques and challenges are not new. The regulations outlined in The Hague Convention have created a lot of intense and complex procedures designed to protect children (although there is not much evidence that it has reduced trafficking). Furthermore, ways to measure the magnitude of children in crisis who might benefit from adoption are varied and conflicted, much like measuring something like poverty. Our point here is to show that there should be caution in examining motivation to adopt, the process of adoption, and raising adopted children. We advocate for caution but also encourage resisting inflated claims that there is no orphan crisis and that evangelical Christians are blatantly taking children without any thought or safeguards. This kind of critique becomes another potential harm in an already complex environment full of children at risk. For more on this, see the salaciously titled, *The Child Catchers: Rescue, Trafficking, and the New Gospel of Adoption* by Kathryn Joyce. This collection of horror stories takes what could have been an important education about familial colonialism and instead feeds into anti-adoption tropes and adoptism—both of which can also harm children.

Adoption, then, is neither good nor bad. It is a tool and a reality for dealing with an unjust and broken world—but at worst it can be an unintentional re-creation of dominant ideologies transmitted through the family unit. Transracially adopted people have to traverse adoption and race and therefore adoptism (privileging a biological family over an adoptive family) and racism.[24] When someone asks about transracial adoption, we suggest thoughtfulness and caution. Moore says, "hesitancy about transracial adoption is so sad."[25] Rather than sad, it is a fundamental part of preventing *familial colonialism*. We use this term to refer to the settling of White epistemologies in the black and brown bodies of children through the avenue and claims of "saving them." The great needs of the world are not alleviated by good intentions. Good intentions can, in fact, exacerbate the world's greatest needs. Our purpose here is to look critically and deeply into the religious motivations of some of the more complicated parts of life and to show that following Jesus is not Whitewashing, but in fact preserving of indigenous cultures, birth culture, epistemologies, and ways of life that exist outside of Europe and North America.

Adoptio Conclusion and a Way Forward

School … forcibly snatches away children from a world of the mystery of God's own handiwork … it is a manufactory specially designed for grinding out uniform results.[26]
—Rabindranath Tagore

We are not anti-missionaries—in fact we are missionaries. We are not anti-adoption—we are adoptive families. We are not anti-education—we are educators. The uncritical and deeply engrained White architecture of salvation and the unchallenged, unchecked, and uncritical approach to White saviorism continues to perpetuate power and dominance through the exploitation of religious and social structures; this is not the way of Jesus. There are no easy remedies for the mass of powers and principalities that work toward these dominant ends, but the act of naming these powers is, for us, an act of resistance. The White architecture of salvation exists inside of us and it works in opposition to Jesus. The absence of a clear solution to complex problems should not prevent the naming of the problems. The cultivation of consciousness and the freedom from oppressive structures established in the name of religion is in fact essential to the life-changing good news at the root of the message of Jesus.

Notes

1. Kipling, Rudyard. *The white man's burden. Rudyard Kipling's verse, inclusive edition, 1885–1918*. Garden City: Doubleday, Page & Co., 1922; Bartleby.com, 2013. Retrieved from www.bartleby.com/364/

2. Image available at: https://commons.wikimedia.org/wiki/File:American_progress.JPG

3. Lili'uokalani. *Hawai'i's Story: By Hawai'i's Queen*. Honolulu, HI: Mutual Publishing, 1990, p. xi.

4. Cook, Christopher L. *The providential life and heritage of Henry Obookiah*. Waimea, HI: Pa'a Studios, 2015.

5. Siler, Julia Flynn. *Lost kingdom: Hawai'i's last queen, the sugar Kings, and America's first imperial adventure*. New York, NY: Grove Press, 2012.

6. Silva, Noenoe K. "Kanawai E Ho'opau I Na Hula Kuolo Hawai'i: The Political Economy of Banning the Hula," *The Hawaiian Journal of History* 34(1): 29–48, 2000.

7. De Sousa Santos, Boaventura. *Epistemologies of the south: Justice against epistemicide*. New York, NY: Routledge, 2016.

8. Pratt, Richard H. "The advantages of mingling Indians with whites." Proceedings of the national conference of Charities and Corrections, 1892, p. 46. Retrieved from https://play.google.com/books/reader?id=dpJIAAAAYAAJ&printsec=frontcover&output=reader&hl=en&pg=GBS.PA45.

9. Pratt, Richard H. Address given to Baptist Convention, 1983. Retrieved from: http://www.nmai.si.edu/education/codetalkers/html/chapter3.html.

10. Pratt, Richard Henry. *Battlefield and classroom: Four decades with the American Indian*. Edited by Rubert M. Utley. New Haven, CT: Yale University Press, 1964.

11. Noriega, Jorge. "American Indian Education in the United States: Indoctrination for Subordination into Colonialism." In *The state of native America*, edited by M. Annette James. Boston, MA: South End Press, 1992, pp. 371–402.

12. Prucha, Francis Paul. *Americanizing the American Indians: Writings by the "Friends of the Indian," 1880–1900*. Cambridge: Harvard University Press, 1973, p. 194.

13. Morgan, Henry Lewis. *Ancient society*. Tucson, AZ: University of Arizona Press, 1985.

14. Lomawaima, K. Tsianina, and Teresa L. McCarty. *To remain an Indian: Lessons in democracy from a century of Native American education*. New York and London: Teachers College Press, 2006.

15. Brown, Lydia X. Z. "Being 'Transracial' Is Real—But It's Not What Racist White People Claim It Is," *Rewire*, January 5, 2018. Retrieved from https://rewire.news/article/2018/01/05/transracial-real-not-racist-white-people-claim/

16. Dei, George J. Sefa, and Agnes M. Calliste. *Power, knowledge and anti-racism education: A critical reader*. Black Point, NS: Fernwood, 2000, p. 11.

17. Shakti. "The Transracial Adopters' Shopping List." In *In search of belonging: Reflections by transracially adopted people*, edited by Perlita Harris. London: British Association for Adoption & Fostering, 2006.

18. Rafferty, Erin. July 24, 2015. Retrieved from https://www.usatoday.com/story/news/nation/2015/07/26/korean-war-orphans/30630161/

19. Moore, Russell. *Adopted for life: The priority of adoption for Christian families and churches*. Wheaton, IL: Crossway, 2015, p. 31.

20. Ibid., p. 35.

21. van Gulden, Holly, and Lisa M. Barels-Rabb. *Real parents, real children: Parenting the adopted child*. New York, NY: Crossroad, 2007, p. 96.

22. Nixon, Ron. "De-Emphasis on Race in Adoption is Criticized," *New York Times*, May 27, 2008, A-15.

23. Moore, 2015, p. 146.
24. Hall, Beth, and Gail Steinberg. *Inside transracial adoption*. London: Jessica Kingsley Publishers, 2000.
25. Ibid.
26. Tagore, Rabindranath. *The English writings of Rabindranath Tagore essays*. New Delhi: Atlantic Publishers, 2007, p. 400.

· 6 ·

WHITENESS IN CHRISTIAN
HIGHER EDUCATION

"What America needs is a return to the old time values that made America great."
That means, in the mainstream of evangelical thought, to go back to the days of
patriarchal, parental, and Protestant supremacy. Contemporary evangelicals would
like to roll back the advances made by the women's and civil rights movements
which have challenged not only the legitimacy of patriarchal authority, but also its
very desirability for women, children, and men of any color, creed, or class.[1]
—*Keeping Them Out of the Hands of Satan* by Susan D. Rose, 1988

Introduction

One byproduct of White Christianity is White Christian higher education.
The advent of church-related colleges has always been a White phenomenon. An examination of key moments in the history of Christian higher education reveals the same kind of White supremacist attitudes and tendencies
that have permeated Christianity from the fifteenth century to today. What
is perhaps most unique in excavating the history of White Christian colleges
is how misguided theology and Christian education have played a critical role
within the larger tapestry of Christian education to lay the foundation for the
proliferation of White Christian higher education institutions.

The White architecture of salvation was formed by White theologians and college founders within the framework of a White European superiority that had permeated Protestant Christianity in the United States by the seventeenth century. Although many highly regarded leaders within the sphere of Christian theological education are considered cornerstones of the teaching of biblical virtues, their contribution is suspect because of the ideology of White dominance. White dominance in Christianity has produced silence around issues of injustice and impotence in creating space for justice work in Christian higher education.

Prominent theologian Willie Jennings has argued that geographical space is also fundamental to addressing Whiteness within Christianity and we would say, by extension, Christian higher education. He has argued that Christians are "geographically adrift" and have almost no understanding about why their organizations and institutions are in their current geographical locations. Jennings says, "What existed in the place before your ... school ... what was there? Who lives around you?"[2] Part of the remembering, repenting, and healing must involve understanding space and location and what drove these institutions to end up where they are today.

This chapter includes a range of topics from demographics in Christian higher education to the underlying racist policies that originally prohibited people of color from enrolling or living on campus. We also examine the history of Christian churches and concomitantly Christian colleges that intentionally moved out of the cities and into the suburbs to sequester themselves from undesirable elements in society.

White Theology and Christian Education

White theology may best be demonstrated by someone who openly holds a White supremacist mindset while simultaneously educating future Christian ministers in seminary. White theology can also be seen in the justification of Christianity's racist past, the rationalization of slavery, and an anti-civil rights theology that continues to permeate the church in America and, by extension, Christian higher education.

Private Christian education at all levels has always been dominantly White. In higher education, the demographics of almost all member institutions within the Council for Christian Colleges & Universities (CCCU), a consortium that represents 115 Christian evangelical universities and colleges in North America, are also largely White. These colleges and universities consistently reflect a greater predominance of White students, faculty, staff, senior administrators, and board members than people of color as compared to public higher education institutions.[3] According to one scholar, "a Christian worldview, more than any other system of thought, dominated American intellectual development during the colonial period."[4] Therefore, early U.S. educational foundations reflected, to some degree, a Christian worldview. The first higher education institutions in the United States, such as Harvard and Yale, were founded with intentional Christian purposes and existed mostly for the purpose of educating future Christian ministers. As these institutions continually became more secularized, the campuses also became more diverse. Leaders of Christian colleges, in their efforts to remain distinctively Christian, found a way to remain distinctively White. The fusion of education and religion also impacted race with White cultural norms as a base of Christianity.

To understand the pervasiveness of whiteness during the forming of Christian education in America, it is important to note that fewer than thirty Black people graduated from college prior to the Civil War.[5] In the post-Civil War South, most Christian schools that trained people for ministry remained segregated. It was not until 1951 that all of the Southern Presbyterian divinity schools were desegregated, and even then, Jim Crow-era admission practices "did not necessarily mean that they were entitled to use all of the facilities of the school immediately."[6] Therefore, during the proliferation of Christian education in America, these "God-honoring" institutions with orthodox theology and a missional purpose granted the opportunity for education almost exclusively to White students. The White theology of those in power played a role in the development and maintenance of exclusionary practices.

Origins of White Christian Higher Education

During a formative White-dominated era of Christian higher education, professors who taught theological education for the training of Christian ministers held White supremacist and racist views. A theologian and pastor, Philip Schaff, was a faculty member at Union Theological Seminary. He exemplified the White supremacist mindset cloaked in biblical theology that permeated Christian higher education in the 1800s in the United States. At first impression, he appears as a White Christian advocate for racial justice. For example, he enthusiastically opposed slavery as evidenced by the argument in his book *Slavery and the Bible: A Tract for the Times.*[7] Schaff wrote that slavery

> takes its rise in sin, and more particularly in war and the law of brute force. Lust of power, avarice and cruelty were the original motives, kidnapping, conquest in war, and purchase by money were the original methods or depriving men of their personal freedom and degrading them to mere instruments for the selfish ends of others ... slaves were born such and were innocently inherited like any other kind of property.[8]

Schaff referenced John Newton's 1813 interpretation of Genesis 9:25 ("Cursed be the *father* of Canaan") and stated that he agreed that Noah's curse was a prophecy regarding the future of Ham's descendants referenced in an earlier chapter of this book. Unlike Newton and others who followed, who understood Noah's prophecy to be a prescription and defense for the institution of slavery, Schaff used Newton's interpretation to argue that this authentic prophecy was a curse that must be lifted. He wrote that "God alone, in his infinite wisdom and mercy, can and will settle the negro question by turning even a curse into a blessing and by overruling the wrath of man for his own glory."[9] The rhetoric corresponds with that of an advocate for freedom and equality, given his opposition to slavery and his trust in the sovereign God to turn even a curse into a blessing.

However, upon closer examination of this text, it is evident that Schaff believed that the curse of slavery was part of God's providence. He also believed slavery was brought about for the sake of discipline upon African peoples, and that the superior White race would be the heroes of the tragedy by freeing enslaved Africans and Christianizing the entire African continent.

Schaff was not alone in his thinking, and many prominent church leaders, theologians, and campus leaders held similar views. This thinking represented a different kind of mindset about racism than the overt racism of slavery and Jim Crow policies in the South. Schaff's racism was a blend of superiority that presented as a liberator of people—similar to the missionary movements discussed in the previous chapter. These leaders were influential in the church and lived according to their interpretation of scripture, which included hierarchical racialized assumptions of superiority. This type of "three-fifths theology"[10] drove the thinking of White Christians in positions of dominance and power. Racism was blatant in Christian education in the South. For example, Black students did not have access to education in most of the theological institutions of higher education until the middle of the twentieth century.[11] Conversely, White Christians in the North had been understood as champions in the fight to end slavery, and Schaff was no exception.

Various ideologies and expressions of White superiority are at the foundation of Christian higher education in the United States. Generations of White students experienced theological formation in classrooms and through mentoring relationships. One of Schaff's students recounted his admiration for his professor:

> To his lectures I listened, as did all his students, with open-mouthed admiration for the encyclopaedic character of his attainments, and, all through my seminary course, there was no one more willing to take minutes from a busy life for the giving of private advice and imparting information than was Dr. Schaff.[12]

His impact was regarded as important in the life of his students and Christian education as a whole. However, Schaff's mindset was one that had been in the making for centuries and that propagated and instilled the notion of White Christian superiority. In the context of Schaff's teaching, his students went on to be pastors, theologians, and professors spreading imbedded notions of White ascendancy through churches, schools, Christian organizations, and missions work throughout the United States and the world. Schaff's views offer a small insight into the proliferation of the White dominant mindset.

White Christian Flight

Whenever we speak at Christian colleges about diversity and justice, a common complaint is often presented. Faculty and staff say they long for diversity on campus, but they say that they have no pipelines in the schools or neighborhood from which to draw students or faculty. This has been a common refrain from White employees who also bemoan the lack of diversity on their campuses. In spite of stated claims to desire diversity, there is a litany of excuses ranging from geography to qualifications to fit. Rarely do White colleagues interrogate the origins of decisions made by some of their institutions' founders. Rarely do we critique the White Christian logic that led to decisions to plant or relocate a campus.

Scholar and theologian Soong-Chan Rah[13] has traveled to many Christian college campuses making the argument that White theology has long been and continues to be one of the seclusion and exclusion of God's people. He contends that the theology of Whiteness formed in the early days of pilgrims on the Mayflower with the intent to be "a city on a hill" in any new community. As many new citizens arrived into the country, they settled into cities. Christians saw their place as a city on a hill to shine their light and be relevant, and they understood this city on a hill in the same way the Israelites related to the city of Jerusalem in the Old Testament of the Bible. This mindset began to shift, however, as more immigrants from the less desirable parts of Europe and around the world began arriving on America's shores. As the Great Migration occurred from the end of the Civil War to the end of World War II, with large numbers of Black citizens leaving the south and rural towns for the cities, many White churches began to flee the cities that they once thought were their new Jerusalem. Instead of Jerusalem, they began to understand the city centers as the biblical equivalent to Babylon—the place of exile to which the Israelites were condemned after their disobedience to God. Just as the Israelites wanted to flee from their Babylon, so White Christians have fled from what they have perceived to be their modern-day Babylon—urban city centers—to the safe havens of the suburbs. In Southern California, Pepperdine, Westmont, and Point Loma all relocated their primary campus away from city centers to ocean-view properties in the midst of turmoil.

Churches followed new communities of White Christians seeking to rebuild the *city on a hill* notions, and as Rah points out, even the physical architecture of churches (inverted arcs from the days of Noah) reflected the ideology of seclusion and protection form the negative elements in surrounding communities. Christian colleges followed suit. Instead of engaging in the diversity of the city, Christian colleges also fled to the suburbs to seclude themselves from the evils of the city. Perhaps this is what drives the "spirituality of the church" theology from some socially conservative denominations that refused to engage in the civil rights movement in the 50s and 60s. Many white church leaders did not see it as the role of the church to be involved in civil matters as they pertained to civil rights and freedom, but these same leaders did not hesitate from actively engaging or being silently complicit in practices that perpetuated Jim Crow legislation.

This mindset of separation from the evils of diversification continued beyond Christian *higher* education to Christian education as a whole, even well after the racial progress of the civil rights movement. One such example, referenced by the quote at the beginning of this chapter, is from Susan Rose who conducted an ethnographic study of two evangelical Christian parochial schools and titled her book, *Keeping Them Out of the Hands of Satan*. Starting with the book's preface, it is clear that the author's perspective of Christian education is partly to separate from racial diversity:

The evangelical cry went out. In the words of Reverend Jerry Falwell, "What America needs is a return to the old time values that made America great." That means, in the mainstream of evangelical thought, to go back to the days of patriarchal, parental, and Protestant supremacy. Contemporary evangelicals would like to roll back the advances made by the women's and civil rights movements which have challenged not only the legitimacy of patriarchal authority, but also its very desirability for women, children, and men of any color, creed, or class. (p. xviii)[14]

Rose argued that "patriarchal authority" had a certain "desirability" for all people including women and people of color that the women's movement and the civil rights movement changed. In other words, she argued that White Christian men have historically known what is best for all other people, but women and people of color have challenged their authority. She went on to say that there had been a "common ground" of patriotism and Christianity that belonged to White evangelical Christians, but that was destroyed "when it expanded to include the interests of other religious, racial, ethnic, and special-interest groups."[15] These concerns were the impetus for Rose's study and provide a clear example of the White supremacy that has permeated Christian education.

Racist Policies, Practices, and Climate

In addition to physically retreating from the evils and temptations of the secular world, fundamentalist Bible colleges created policies that upheld racist mindset and syncretistically amalgamated it into a distorted brand of White Christianity in America. The penultimate goal for many Christian colleges was to maintain traditional family and religious values that were in danger of being watered down. In an era of religious freedom this may indeed be a worthy endeavor. However, the application and syncretism embedded in White Christianity revealed both intended and unintended consequences. One such college is Bob Jones University (BJU). Founded in 1927 in Florida and later moved to South Carolina, the university excluded Black students from attendance until 1975. While single Black students were admitted, the university continued to forbid interracial dating on campus until a policy change in 2000. White evangelist Bob Jones, from whom the university gets its name, believed that Black people should be grateful to White people for bringing them out of Africa while enslaved. Otherwise, they may have remained unconverted.[16]

Other Bible colleges and Christian universities across the country have historically enrolled, and with a few exceptions continue to enroll, low numbers of Black students. Again, as many of these campuses are in rural and dominantly white areas of the country, students of color will not feel a sense of belonging either on the college campus or in the surrounding communities.

The Religious White and Christian Higher Education

In a previous chapter we discussed the role of politics and the Religious White. Some of the most ardent supporters of the Religious White have been leaders of Christian higher education institutions. Bob Jones University and Liberty University have had unapologetic political connections to the Republican Party, with President Trump offering his first commencement address at Liberty University[17] and asking its president, Jerry Falwell Jr., to lead a regulations reform task force for the White House.[18] Education leaders in these conservative settings often view social and racial justice with suspicion because of its potential connection to liberalism. The same Jerry Falwell Jr. responded to a 2015 mass shooting in San Bernardino California with a statement about preemptively killing Muslims. At a chapel service on the Liberty University campus a few days after the shooting, Falwell stated that "If some of those people in that community center had what I have in my back pocket right now ... is it illegal to pull it out? I don't know." Falwell chuckled as he made this statement, over roars of applause from the student body. He went on to state the need for preemptive measures for Muslims: "I've always thought that if more good people had concealed-carry permits, then we could end those Muslims before they walked in ... and killed them."[19] In this moment, the role of gun violence, the right to own guns according to the Second Amendment, and the overlapping beliefs in the authority of the Constitution and the Bible emerged.

The student experience on dominantly White campuses has been characterized by the degree to which students feel as though they belong. For students of color, this issue has been exacerbated on dominantly White Christian campuses. Numerous articles and dissertations have shown the degree of difficulty students of color face when trying to navigate a dominantly White space that is infused with the White architecture of salvation. This is especially prominent for Christian students who were raised in a predominantly Asian, Latino, or Black Church and attend a college with the expectation that their spiritual needs will be met. Some studies found that the path to spiritual growth for White students and Christian institutions was characterized by a sense of satisfaction—put differently, "Have all of my expectations been met?"[20] For students of color, the path to spiritual growth was characterized by a sense of belonging—put differently, "Have I found a seat at the table?"

Professor Jarvis Williams offered several ways that Christian colleges can confront White supremacy on campus. He includes:

- Don't make excuses for the racism of certain heroes of the Christian faith
- Don't make political ideology a mark of Christian or institutional identity
- Don't be color blind
- Read and require black and brown author
- Intentionally pursue qualified black and brown people to fill positions with "real" institutional power and privilege[21]

As Christian campuses continue to find Nazi symbols and n[word] written on cars, nooses hanging from trees, and students, faculty, and staff of color ostracized and aggressed, these five suggestions are poignant beginnings for taking apart the structures of Whiteness that have been given sacred status.

Evangelical White Out

As educators who work on Christian higher education campuses, we understand that painful racialized incidents occur with regularity around the country, and even at our own institutions. One does not have to look far to find them. We offer the following two scenarios to capture the challenges associated with efforts to address the dominance of Whiteness in Christian higher education. One example of a chilly campus climate came in a 2018 *Relevant Magazine*[22] article focused on Moody Bible Institute (MBI) in Chicago. Former and current students told stories of White dominance and institutional resistance at their mostly White Christian campus: racist jokes about Rodney King and police brutality, nooses hung around cutouts of famous Black actor Will Smith, and other passing comments from students followed by silence from other students and faculty. These experiences served as evidence of a chilly climate for many former students of color. Even typical or normal Christian events were embedded with a culture of Whiteness. The required chapel services, for instance, were culturally White with Black gospel songs predictably incorporated on Black History Month and special services. However, the example that garnered the most attention was from the faculty.

A theology professor at Moody, Bryan Litfin is someone who represents Christian faculty who are deniers of racism, and vocal critics of diversity initiatives at Moody and other faith-based institutions. He, like many other White colleagues at Christian institutions in America, holds to the belief that the term "White privilege" is "offensive on its face and unworthy of Christian discourse."[23] He has written an article arguing against such language and criticized a student group seeking to right the wrongs of racialized events on the campus.

At Biola University in Southern California in 2017, a disgruntled White male Christian administrator sued the dominantly White conservative evangelical college for racial discrimination.[24] In the lawsuit, the plaintiff alleges that in the push for diversity, the university president and key senior leaders intentionally excluded White men and hired an under-qualified person of color. In the fall of the same 2017 academic year, a distinguished professor of philosophy in Biola's Talbot School of Theology, J. P. Moreland, wrote an article bemoaning that the diversity–social justice–White privilege (DSW) movement is an ongoing use of secular, leftist, neo-Marxist terms such as White privilege. He further argues that Christians ought to "think biblically and carefully about the contemporary DSW movement."[25] These cautionary tales of faculty members who are critical of equity scholarship are reminiscent of the prevailing theology and writings of early Christian college founders warning against the dangers of secularism and slippery slopes. While it is easy to highlight these two institutions here, our analysis is not simply to focus on any one institution, because the power of Whiteness is not contained in any one single institution. We argue that Whiteness is a system of dominance embedded in the architecture of all institutions and therefore future examples will inevitably emerge on other campuses. These concerns about diversity are a common refrain heard throughout the history of Christian institutions of higher learning in the U.S., and the rhetoric has the potential to dismiss racial justice and equity movements for people of color and offer students at Christian institutions a miseducation in identity and justice.

Roots and Fruits

We have seen the common and at-times predictable responses to racial incidents on Christian colleges from their presidents. The expressions vary slightly, but by and large they state how the actions and behaviors of a few do not reflect the character, mission, or values of the overall institution. It is the "bad apple" theory and it has run rampant as a poor excuse for racist acts on Christian college campuses. The same is certainly true for their secular counterparts. The bad apple theory focuses solely on individual actions and fails to recognize the deeper and broader systemic issues that cultivate the behavior. Why focus on the fruit, and not recognize the branches, the roots, the soil, and the very life-giving ecosystem that fostered, formed, and bore the fruit? Rarely will one hear a president own the problem and simply state that the actions are a result of an institutional problem in which everyone is in some way complicit. Our challenge to our fellow colleagues serving at Christian colleges is to embrace the whole covenant theology that is rooted in the Gospel. God saves individuals but also saves his covenant people, something a Western white culture struggles to understand and embrace.

A Way Forward

A group of White Christians once challenged the White evangelical status quo and called White evangelicals to engage in social activism (including combating racial hatred) as part of their Christian commitment. In the early 1920s these neo-evangelicals began shifting away from the strict fundamentalism that was in itself a response to a liberal movement within certain Protestant traditions. The neo-evangelicals espoused to an engagement with—rather than a separation from—the prevailing culture, which they believed was necessary for effective evangelism. They sought to become more deeply engaged in the present social evils, including combating racial hatred, and they sought to impact Christian higher education.[26] Some like-minded individuals continue to work toward social change within Christian higher education, but are often dismissed at best as Social Justice Warriors who have bought into the ways of the world, or worse, accused of socialism, Marxism, and liberalism—terms tantamount to being unbiblical and therefore worthy of discipline or removal from the fold.

Just as the mid-twentieth-century neo-evangelical scholars in Christian higher education were summoning White Christians to take seriously their role in addressing racial problems, so we are asking the same response from Christian higher education leaders today. We propose that a way forward for Christian higher education involves understanding the racial connections to their theological foundations and geographical locations. Christian higher education leaders must understand the past and present racial injustices from a Christian theological perspective. If institutional leaders do not begin and end with their own fundamental theological grounding as a way to dismantle racial dominance from their institutions, changes will continue to be nearly impossible. In other words, Christian higher education must understand that Christian theology is at the center of racial justice, and racial justice is at the center of Christian theology.

Institutional leaders must also tell the truth about Whiteness and their institutions. An uncomfortable truth about the lies of White superiority in the history of Christian higher education needs to be exposed. Christian history classes must include the troubling facts that we have outlined in this book with regard to the fusion of White domination and Christianity. Christian colleges and universities that purposefully withheld admission from Black students, prohibited the full inclusion of Black students in community life, and have based their institutions' theological grounding on theologians who published works on the inferiority of Blacks must tell and own their histories through courses and public events. Christian colleges should find statues and documents that reveal their racist histories and place them in museums so that we can see and learn about the racism that was once on public display but is now commonly hidden within the hearts and unconscious minds of people. These museums could serve as a way to educate about the past and inspire hope about the possibility of a new future. Educational leaders must guide their communities through the processes of remembering, repenting, and healing.

Notes

1. Rose, Susan D. *Keeping them out of the hands of Satan: Evangelical schooling in America.* New York, NY: Routledge, 1988.
2. Jennings, Willie J. *Can "White" People Be Saved?* [Video file], November, 2017. Retrieved from https://www.youtube.com/watch?v=9wRvaG9j53g
3. Reyes, R., and K. Case. "National Profile on Ethnic/Racial Diversity of Enrollment, Graduation Rates, Faculty, and Administrators among the CCCU," 2011. Retrieved from http://citl.goshen.edu/cccu-report; Rine, P. J., and D. S. Guthrie. "Return to Justice: Six Movements that Reignited Our Contemporary Evangelical Conscience," *Christian Higher Education* 15(1–2): 4–23, 2016. doi:10.1080/1536750.2016.1107347.
4. Ringenberg, William C. *The Christian college: A history of Protestant higher education in America.* 2nd ed. Grand Rapids, MI: Renewed Minds, 2006.
5. Ibid.
6. Reimers, David M. 1965. *White Protestantism and the Negro.* New York, NY: Oxford University Press.
7. Schaff, David Schley. *The life of Philip Schaff: In part autobiographical.* New York, NY: Charles Scribner's Sons, 1897.
8. Schaff, Phillip. *Slavery and the Bible: A tract for the times.* Chambersburg, PA: M. Kieffer & Co's Caloric Printing Press, 1861.

9. Ibid., p. 3.

10. Tait, Lewis T., and A. Christian Van Gorder. *Three-fifths theology: Challenging racism in American Christianity*. Trenton, NJ: Africa World Press, 2002.

11. Reimers, 1965.

12. Schaff, 1897, p. 292.

13. Rah, Soong-Chan. "SL Value Series: Diversity." Filmed [February, 2018]. YouTube video, 36 minutes. Posted [February 20, 2018]. Retrieved from https://www.youtube.com/watch?v=A8QlJcHHbVc&feature=youtu.be

14. Rose, 1988, p. xviii.

15. Ibid., p. 31.

16. "Blacks Still Not Wanted at Many Christian Colleges," *The Journal of Blacks in Higher Education*, No. 17 (Autumn, 1997), pp. 79–82.

17. "Read President Trump's Liberty University Commencement Speech," *Time*, May 13, 2017. Retrieved from http://time.com/4778240/donald-trump-liberty-university-speech-transcript/

18. Blumenstyk, Goldie. "A Task Force with Falwell Is Happening, White House Says," *The Chronicle of Higher Education*, June 11, 2017. Retrieved from https://www.chronicle.com/article/A-Task-Force-With-Falwell-Is/240315.

19. Baily, Sarah Pulliam. "Jerry Falwell Jr.: 'If More Good People had Concealed-Carry Permits, then We Could End Those' Islamist Terrorists," *Washington Post*, December 5, 2015. Retrieved from https://www.washingtonpost.com/news/acts-of-faith/wp/2015/12/05/liberty-university-president-if-more-good-people-had-concealed-guns-we-could-end-those-muslims/?utm_term=.0c4e7d88cdf4.

20. Paredes-Collins, Kristin, and Christopher S. Collins. "A Study of Underrepresented Students' Spiritual Development at Predominantly White Evangelical Colleges." *Journal of Research on Christian Higher Education* 20: 73–100, 2011; Paredes-Collins, Kristin. "Campus Climate for Diversity as a Predictor of Spiritual Development at Christian Colleges." *Religion & Education* 41(2): 171–193, 2014.

21. Williams, Jarvis. "5 Ways Christian Institutions of Higher Education Can Avoid White Supremacy," *The Witness*, December 1, 2016. Retrieved March 15, 2018 from https://thewitnessbcc.com/5-ways-christian-institutions-higher-education-can-avoid-white-supremacy/

22. Merritt, Jonathan. "How White Privilege is Destroying One of America's Oldest Bible Colleges," *Relevant Magazine*, January 22, 2018. Retrieved from https://relevantmagazine.com/current/white-privilege-destroying-one-americas-oldest-bible-colleges/

23. Ibid.

24. "'Diversity' Push Explodes Life of White Christian Rising Star," *WorldNetDaily* (WND), October 15, 2017. Retrieved from wnd.com/2017/10/diversity-madness-explodes-life-of-white-christian-rising-star/.

25. Moreland, James Porter. "Christians, The Diversity-Social Justice-White Privilege Movement, and What It's Got To Do with Real Love," December 6, 2017. Retrieved from https://www.christianpost.com/voice/christians-the-diversity-social-justice-white-privilege-movement-and-what-its-got-to-do-with-real-love.html.

26. Henry, Carl F. H. *The uneasy conscience of modern fundamentalism*. Grand Rapids, MI: Wm. B. Eerdmans Publishing, 1947.

· 7 ·

WHITE WORSHIP

I can't imagine anything but music that could have brought about this alchemy.
Maybe it's because music is about as physical as it gets: your essential rhythm is your
heartbeat; your essential sound, the breath. We're walking temples of noise, and
when you add tender hearts to this mix, it somehow lets us meet in places we couldn't
get to any other way.

—Anne Lamott[1]

Introduction

In irreverent musings, Anne Lamott describes her journey of faith and how
she ended up in church. A White woman in recovery from alcohol and drug
addiction, Lamott recounts how initially, it was not the preaching or the
church's social justice efforts that led her to the gospel. Instead, Lamott writes,
"it was the singing that pulled me in and split me wide open."[2]

Worship music can serve as a powerful expression of faith that touches
people at the deepest levels of human existence—psychologically, emotionally, spiritually, and in embodied ways. It also conveys symbolic meaning and
mirrors society's cultural norms. In the dominantly White U.S. church and
social context, worship music often conceals power. The embedded cultural

norms and sense of connection many White Americans feel in worship translate to ease, familiarity, and comfort that normalizes Whiteness and equates White worship with innate rightness and convincingly, perceived neutrality. For many people of color in dominantly White religious spaces, White worship is another feature of the racial status hierarchy we negotiate every day. White worship signifies the ominous relationship between Whiteness, culture, and power that many White congregants fail to notice or ever question.

Distinctive and culturally relevant worship styles have evolved over time and in important ways across multiple religious contexts, such as predominantly Black and Korean churches. One unique expression of religious hegemony, however, is the exercise of White dominance through music and worship—the belief in an inherent and ontological *rightness* in *Whiteness*. In this way, White worship functions to reinscribe the White architecture of salvation. Furthermore, the field of ethnomusicology offers some helpful tools and perspectives on the study of music from the perspective of multiple cultures. In this chapter, we discuss the expansion of Christianity in Korea, the evolution of worship in Black American settings, and worship practices in dominantly White Christian higher education.

Decolonizing Music in Korea

Soong-Chan Rah addressed concerns about the dominantly White norms of Western missionary practices in *The Next Evangelicalism*[3] and critiqued the lack of cultural criticality in the mindsets of Western missionaries who go abroad to evangelize. One way to understand the White architecture of salvation and the function of White dominance is to consider how Western missionaries from North America brought White worship to Korea.

By way of example, the first missionaries to Korea in the late 1800s came from North America. Often motivated by the desire to spread their faith, these missionaries were culturally myopic and unable to distinguish between the essence of spiritual faith and cultural power. When White Western missionaries first heard Koreans play music on the pentatonic scale (a five-note scale that Westerners would recognize as equivalent to the five black notes on the piano), they interpreted the music as unchristian. Western missionaries, after all, wrote worship songs based on diatonic major scales, the seven-note scale that is the basis for most Western music. When North American missionaries first heard musical notes in Korea, their White Western captivity[4] likely constrained their spiritual imagination. Failing to acknowledge the cultural dominance embedded within their own practices, Western missionaries categorized Korean music, which adopted the pentatonic scale common throughout Asia, as unregenerate. In other words, the diatonic style that was more familiar to White Western missionaries sounded and felt more *Christian* to them. It is also worth observing the racialized symbolism embedded in the keys. For White Western missionaries, white keys represented what was *holy* while the black keys symbolized what needed *redemption*. Most of the musical traditions in Africa, Asia, and other parts of the Global South are pentatonic. They punctuate the black keys. Undoubtedly, Western missionaries assigned religious significance to their musical practices. It is important to note that by the late-nineteenth century, pentatonicism was popular in Western vernacular music. The song *Amazing Grace* is a notable example. Some might argue that there is no basis for assigning a dualistic significance to white and black keys, since everything not written in C major or A minor would need to use black keys. Furthermore, White missionaries would have been suspicious of the exclusive pattern of pentatonicism, since it was alien to their dominant cultural expressions in Western Protestant music. White missionaries, after all, were consistently committed to colonialist ideologies that obscured their judgment.

Why did Western missionaries to Korea allow primarily American/English Protestant music when starting churches in Korea? This topic is important to understanding church history and the expansion of world missions, which is paralleled elsewhere around the world. The example of Korea is important for several reasons, not least of which is that many Korean evangelicals align with mainline American evangelicalism and have also influenced it.

Secondly, among ethnomusicologists, there has been longstanding, vigorous discussion and scholarship about missionaries and music. Hyun Kyong Chang's ethnographic study interrogated the role of music and Christianity in Korea.[5] Chang addressed how cultural imperialism ultimately shaped music in the Korean church and why Western Christian music was so readily adopted in Korea. Chang and others[6] have argued that western missionaries not only brought Protestantism as a new religion to Korea; they brought Western ideologies of democracy, modernity, and nationalism.

Western missionaries originally introduced English hymns, such as *Amazing Grace*, *A Mighty Fortress*, and *Old Rugged Cross* to Korean churches. English hymns are central features of Korean hymnals today to the point that some Korean Christians think of the hymns as Korean. I (Jun) recall a time when a recent immigrant from South Korea was pleasantly surprised to learn that Christians in American churches also sang hymns by American composer Fanny J. Crosby. By the late-nineteenth century, western composers (most famously Claude Debussy) began experimenting with pentatonicism as a marker of exoticism. Missionaries to Korea around 1900 would not have known this. Yet, Debussy's move exoticized Asians and further complicated the history of pentatonicism.

This cultural and religious fusion became an internalized colonial hermeneutic that informed the way Christians attempted to change new converts in the Global South. When missionaries led people to faith and declared that they were a "new creation," they encouraged the new converts to praise their new God with holy "Christian" music. Western Protestant music was perhaps the only music the missionaries felt was spiritually appropriate. Lyrics were set to popular bar tunes at the time and, ironically, were used to encourage Christians to join in congregational singing.

Martin Luther is credited for sparking the Protestant Reformation. Luther was a pioneer of vernacularism, making esoteric theological jargon more accessible in the worship service—even through music. In the sixteenth century, the Catholic Mass consisted of priests and choirs chanting and singing musical liturgies mostly in Latin.[7] As part of Luther's intended reform of the Catholic church, he sought to have the entire congregation participate in worship rather than a select few. Luther "passed the vocal torch from the officers of the service to the participants, thus elevating congregational singing to a significant place in the worship service."[8] To Luther, simply adding congregational songs into the mix of worship was not the complete solution; he insisted that the worship service be conducted in the vernacular. Luther stated, "It would be reasonable and useful if we used German where most of the people do not understand Latin. Then the people would better understand what is sung or read."[9] In fact, Luther translated many hymns from Latin into German and composed German songs to accompany liturgical texts. He also used the tunes of German songs from the Middle Ages along with original lyrics to write music for liturgical purposes.[10] One scholar credited Luther with "freeing the hymn from its shackling Latinity and developing a vernacular hymnody more on the lines of German folk song."[11]

The result of these changes to the Catholic Mass was a worship style that was reflective of the culture of those in worship. Luther wanted the Mass to elicit worshippers' full participation, and this ideal affected protestant worship throughout history. Some of Luther's hymns may have originated from popular bar tunes in an effort to make the music accessible to the people. While Luther wanted the music to be accessible, he did not get his way in the case of the Catholic Church. Indeed, Mass was conducted in Latin until Vatican II, and the German Lutheran church eventually instituted some of these reforms in the centuries after Luther. For example, Bach's cantatas were sung in German but still performed partially by a choir and soloists.

However, when the missionary work of European Christians in the nineteenth century intermingled with the subjugation of people groups, musical style became part of the colonization package. The Western European hymn eventually became a marker of religious superiority and a sign of true Christian conversion. Music in the east and other regions became colonized to the extent that when Koreans converted Christianity, they ostensibly divorced themselves from their culture and embraced Western music to praise God. What originated as an effort to produce full participation in Christian worship in culturally-familiar language became a style of worship that did the opposite—the musical style itself became a tool of oppression that negatively impacted a people's culture and heritage.

We argue, drawing from ethnomusicology, that when culture is taken away, silenced, or destroyed, at some point a new culture evolves that likely incorporates some of the values of the oppressed people groups. Sometimes an oppressed culture influences the dominant culture and a new form emerges. Hip hop is an example of a musical genre that currently holds a global audience and a musical lingua franca, while country music is not. In this example, however, it is important to observe how hip hop music emerged as a form of relief from oppression, increased in popularity and became mainstream. The music would become susceptible to appropriation and commercialization by the dominant group. Indeed, long before modern generations of teenagers returned from youth retreats to throw away their CD collections of Duran Duran, Pink Floyd, Nirvana, or Eminem, newly converted Christians in Asia gave up their heritage-rich cultural music for the likes of John Wesley, Isaac Watts, and Fanny J. Crosby.

We acknowledge the unique predicament that missionaries may have struggled with to varying degrees in the early days of the Korean church. Although it is true that an old music was replaced by a new music, when White Western missionaries came to the shores of the *Land of Morning Calm*, there was no existing Christian worship music of any kind. This meant that Western missionaries were left with one of two options: bring in American Christian worship music comprehensively or encourage new Korean Christians to write their own worship music. Under colonialist ideology, the latter solution was not plausible to the early missionaries. Although this does not excuse early missionary activity, it may offer some insight into the process by which it all happened. Although Christianity was Whitewashed by Western European expansion, so were Christian rituals, rights, and sacraments.

Amazing Grace

John Newton's *Amazing Grace*, written in 1779, is perhaps the most well-known Christian hymn that has successfully crossed over into the secular music world. Newton's personal testimony is perhaps equally familiar to many Christians. A ship captain of a slave-trading vessel who felt the conviction of the sinfulness of human trafficking, Newton wrote several verses of the hymn to address an awakening that led him spiritually from "blindness" to "sight," from condemnation to salvation. What is lesser known about the hymn is that the musical arrangement is entirely based on the pentatonic scale, raising the question, how did the lyrics eventually become associated with the tune of the hymn? The pentatonic scale was not unique to Western Europeans like Newton who was born and raised in the suburbs of London. As an enslaver, perhaps Newton overheard the tunes of enslaved Africans during their forced travel to the *New World*. Might the tune have been influenced by Africans, only later to be co-opted and appropriated to form a famous hymn? Again, the melody was not set to lyrics until the 1830s or 1840s. At the time, melodies often had lives of their own, and, for that reason, had their own names. Although the piece was originally entitled "New Britain," it does not mean that the tune was not derived from African music. We do not know. Some might contest the argument that pentatonicism has African origins, since there are many examples of pentatonicism in early American secular music.

Fiddle music may be a key to unlocking the mystery of pentatonic origins. There is the possibility that even the pentatonicism in White fiddle traditions came from Black fiddle traditions. There is a good deal of evidence that before 1861, many enslaved Africans played the fiddle and that many tunes in the nineteenth-century American fiddle repertoire were composed or developed by Black players. In the end, perhaps it is too grand a claim to suggest that "New Britain" was taken from African American culture. One reason it may have been popular among Black congregations for the past one hundred years is its pentatonicism, which would overlap with some African music that then influenced the music Africans made when they arrived. Furthermore, the melody may have been sung in a time of great turmoil and misery for enslaved Africans. It was not a happy tune, but rather, a deeply elegiac dirge that expressed tremendous melancholy. Musical colonization runs deep when considering how the most famous of all Christian hymns may be a stolen African song of lament.

Newton may have appropriated Black musical influence when writing one of the most famous hymns of all time, *Amazing Grace*. Pentatonicism has been in Western music since the Middle Ages (some church chants are pentatonic), and many early American tunes are pentatonic (many of the them published by the early 1800s). Contemporary interpretations do not show agreement among scholars. The case of Black and White worship music in the U.S. is complex. The Korean context is just as complex, but I (Jun) am more familiar with what happened in the U.S. over the last 200 years. Africans brought their own music, which was partially preserved and syncretized with European forms. Of course, Black Americans wrote new music that addressed the uniqueness of their cultural, economic, social, and spiritual context. They were taught Anglo hymns, but also came up with their own songs (the spirituals).

Black Church Musical Tradition

Music in Black Christian churches has evolved over time through the migration and evolution of West African styles, which were influenced by oppression and segregation. White Protestant denominations typically maintain a style that is characterized by a strict rule of hymns, psalms, and spiritual songs. There are movements that have counteracted this more *traditional* style that draw from notions of *charisma*, but the rigid style is most characteristic of historic White Christian worship. In the seventeenth and eighteenth centuries, exposure to Christianity and the conversion of enslaved Africans were moral imperatives for White Europeans.

In the northern U.S., enslaved people were located closer to their enslavers, whereas in the southern U.S., they were situated much farther away. Therefore, in the South, there was a greater ability to cultivate a worship style without the surveillance of enslavers. In the nineteenth century, revival meetings were held at camps and the African musical roots were evidenced in the practices of enslaved Africans. Music within the assembly included shouting, jumps, dancing, and other actions that were criticized by mainstream

Christianity, but provided evidence that a Black tradition of music had evolved and was founded on West African conventions like spontaneity and aesthetic appeal.[12] Christianity spread quickly throughout the enslaved South, and plantation owners ended up building houses and sponsoring Black preachers to carry on the establishment—which also led to Black styles of improvisation, flexibility, and reflections of African traditions that spread throughout Black Christianity in the U.S. In the contemporary setting of Black Christianity, distinct Black style exists separately from White hymnody. Renditions of songs vary greatly. Call and response in singing along with quality, tone, and mechanics reflect traditions of Black culture and customs.[13]

The context and experience of Black Christian worship has been critiqued in a variety of ways for reflecting the White architecture of salvation. Malcolm X, for example, remarked in a speech:

> My mother was a Christian and my father was a Christian, and I used to hear them when I was a little child sing songs, "Washing me white as snow." My father was a black man and my mother was a black woman, and yet the songs that they sang in church were designed to fill their hearts with the desire to be white.[14]

In agreement with Malcolm X, perhaps the language of washing and becoming clean should be separated from becoming White. Not only does such language exist, but images of a "lily white Jesus, which was a master-slave hand-me-down from the white church during slavery" are still displayed in some black churches "preventing the masses of black Christians from breaking free of psychic and spiritual bondage that prevents self-esteem, self-identity, and self-determination."[15] For example, when hymnody flows from and stays true to the lament language found in the Psalms, the idea of breaking free becomes more attainable and more biblical. The Psalms are a collection of worship songs and chants used by the ancient Hebrews, and laments are the most frequent type of psalm found in the collection.

Many lament psalms are not used in Christian liturgies. Consider Psalm 137 (NIV), which is a violent psalm of exile:

> [1] By the rivers of Babylon we sat and wept
>   when we remembered Zion.
> [2] There on the poplars
>   we hung our harps,
> [3] for there our captors asked us for songs,
>   our tormentors demanded songs of joy;
>   they said, "Sing us one of the songs of Zion!"

[4] How can we sing the songs of the Lord
   while in a foreign land?
[5] If I forget you, Jerusalem,
   may my right hand forget its skill.
[6] May my tongue cling to the roof of my mouth
   if I do not remember you,
   if I do not consider Jerusalem
   my highest joy.
[7] Remember, Lord, what the Edomites did
   on the day Jerusalem fell.
"Tear it down," they cried,
   "tear it down to its foundations!"
[8] Daughter Babylon, doomed to destruction,
   happy is the one who repays you
   according to what you have done to us.
[9] Happy is the one who seizes your infants
   and dashes them against the rocks.

Ada Maria Isasi-Diaz wrote about this psalm with specific relevance from a Cuban perspective. Her experience and reflection on the psalm highlights her memories of Cuba like the psalmist does Zion, but Isasi-Diaz also affirms that "injustice and oppression are also 'places' of exile."[16] She cites Brueggemann and his works on disorientation to be understood as "pouring out laments and appeals for those for whom the orderly world has fallen apart, for those who doubt the meaning of their ordinary lives."[17] For Brueggemann, the lament is purposely a purging of the soul to allow trouble to be expressed. Through the eyes of Isasi-Diaz, the experience of minoritized peoples can specifically utilize lament as a cry for vengeance in their current situation of exile, giving voice to an authentic experience.[18]

The notions of exile and social control are essential to fully understand the experience of Isasi-Diaz and the intensity of Psalm 137. The "songs of Zion" or praise songs that thank God are the most commonly-used psalms. However, such usage can "articulate and maintain a 'sacred canopy' under which the community of faith can live out its life with freedom from anxiety."[19] These psalms not only serve as the "sacred canopy," but also function as a "form of social control."[20] Social control is a threat when psalms of praise are sung in times of distress. It is the act of taking feelings of oppression and powerlessness and Whiting them out. It is an attempt to "directly legitimate the particular institutional order in question" and "provide the poor with a meaning for their poverty, but also provide the rich with a meaning for their wealth."[21] It is an erasure of pain. Theodicy or religious legitimation dissolves a true connection to God through lament and legitimates even terrifying or painful events by putting them under "the sheltering canopy of the nomos [that] extends to cover even those experiences that may reduce the individual to howling animality."[22] Stephen McCutchan puts the phenomenon anecdotally:

> Praise without lament is like relating to a person who always says positive things but never utters a critical remark. After a while, the praise takes on a false tone. Consider another case. A child gets sick and her parents pray for her recovery … When death comes the parents are cautioned that they should not blame God for their loss. But if they follow this advice, what then can be said of their praise of God? How honest can they be in their worship if they do not acknowledge to God their disappointment and anger that their prayers were not answered?[23]

The loss of lament can eliminate or silence experiences and perspectives in the community of faith.

Perhaps Psalm 137 as a lament has pertinent parallels that speak to White dominance in religion and the social location of Black America. Black literature has dealt with theodicy to some degree, as in Alice Walker's *The Color Purple* when Celie says of God: "Let 'im hear me, I say. If he ever listened to poor colored women the world would be a different place, I can tell you."[24] W. E. B. Du Bois in a seemingly similar tone says: "Keep not Thou Silent, O God! … Surely you, too, art not white, O Lord, a pale bloodless, heartless thing!"[25] This is certainly reminiscent of lament language in Psalm 137 and others specifically giving voice to trials in Black America. Carefully listening to Black spirituals (sometimes called "Negro spirituals"), which were songs composed by African Americans in the nineteenth century and often based on psalms of lament, reveals the spirituals as a way of coding resistance to slavery and suffering. They bear characteristics that are different from traditional hymnody, and contain lots of repetition and are sometimes pentatonic.

Normativity of White Worship in Christian Colleges

Given that we have addressed Whiteness in Christian colleges and universities, we also note that the normativity of White Western Christian music continues today. In 2013, Chris Tomlin's video, "How Great is Our God," went viral. Different people groups around the world were filmed singing versions of the song translated in their native languages. Many supported the video as the ultimate example of Christian unity while others were quick to point out that this was yet another example of what Christian colonial Whitewashing sounds like.

In that same year, a group of White church leaders convened a panel discussion from a conference sponsored by the National Center for Family Integrated Churches (NCFIC).[26] The panel featured White clergy who argued hip hop music was a detrimental form of worship music. Much of the discussion centered on the perceived irreverence that surrounded the style of music. It is helpful to reflect on the importance of understanding the differences of cultural norms from biblical norms. As Carl and Karen Ellis stated in 2013: "We all have a tendency to confuse cultural norms with Biblical ones; yet this is especially harmful when done by the dominant culture of any society."[27]

Christian colleges and universities in the United States also employ musical styles in their student chapel services that reflect a dominance of White Western Christian music. In a chapel service at a dominantly White institution of higher education, it is not unusual to see the same kind of worship band configuration playing the same musical style and playing the same songs as one would find at a White evangelical church on a Sunday morning. Occasionally, some Christian colleges may offer an *alternative* form of worship, such as Gospel night or international chapel in which the music selections may include hip hop styles, rap, or songs sung in Spanish or Swahili. Sometimes songs will be translations of popular praise songs from artists in mainstream Christian labels. Sometimes songs might even be indigenous to a region or country. In either case these *alternative* worship services are subtle reminders of the irregular, non-normative nature that is counter to the dominant Christian culture on faith-based campuses across the country. This reality is particularly problematic for students of color since spirituality is such an important part of the learning process in college. Yet, people across racial groups experience spirituality and spiritual growth differently.[28] One study in particular revealed that when students experienced spiritual discord based on the dominant White culture of a campus, their intent to complete their degree actually diminished.[29] It is worth considering that leaders in higher education who plan chapels that reflect only a White evangelical culture may be colonizing students in the same way that missionaries colonized new converts in the Global South through stripping away the cultural dimensions of their spiritual expression. When institutions make chapel attendance a requirement, this phenomenon is only worsened because the college or university communicates the importance of something (i.e., mandatory attendance) that may actually hinder students' ability to graduate (i.e., creating a spiritually discordant atmosphere).

Worship Normativity and Paradox

People often fail to recognize that religion and culture are inextricably inter-twined. A dangerous result of not recognizing this reality is the possibility of dominant cultural religious practices overpowering spiritual expressions by dismissing them as not truly *Christian*. In the book *The Elusive Dream*, Korie Edwards presented the research she conducted in an interracial church. Edwards described the book as a "journey toward understanding how race manages to control, infuse, and reorganize human relations, such that White remain dominant, even in places that embrace racial diversity."[30] Edwards found that in an interracial setting where the leadership was both Black and White, the church was only integrated racially when Whites were comfort-able with the style of worship. Edwards concluded, "Whiteness plays a critical role in how interracial churches are organized, ultimately producing churches that reflect a congregational life more commonly seen in white church than in others."[31] According to Edwards, not much has changed from the time that White Christian missionaries went to Korea in the 1800s to today.

Another example is that in some Christian Reformed circles, most nota-bly Calvinist and Anabaptist traditions, the Regulative Principle of Wor-ship (RPW) guides church traditions. The regulative principle of worship is understood as a guide for churches to conduct public worship services with specific elements that are found in Bible. An extension of this principle would apply to the prohibition of any practices that are strictly prohibited in scripture. Church leaders and denominations that are guided by the RPW would study and test various aspects of worship based on practices that are explicitly commanded by God, and anything not explicitly articulated should be avoided in public worship. This governing guideline of public worship outlines some specific elements that are deemed appropriate for God-glorify-ing public worship.

Counter to the regulative principle of worship, some denominational leaders hold to a normative principle of worship, which suggests that any-thing that is not prohibited in Scripture may be permissible in public worship, insofar as the practices are both amenable to the larger group and maintain purity and peace within a given congregation. These countering guidelines are offered here to acknowledge that worship wars have been a part of the Christian tradition for generations, and many a member has left a congrega-tion for a perceived violation of either principle. The underlying assumption in these positions is the desire to please God in worship, but often unchecked are the long-held and often invisible interactions with cultural norms and values that typically guide decisions.

Conclusion

Common associations of the terms Christian, White, and American need a deeper critical interrogation in the church and by extension, Christian higher education. This equation is a part of the idolatrous myth and formula that many Christians in the U.S. seem to live by. For many, an underlying fourth element is *Republican*. This equation seems to have been a successful formula for White American Christianity in the U.S. for the past several decades. The *White architecture of salvation*, discussed in the introductory chapter of the book, was designed by the collective dominant mindset of many centuries that is now pervasive in the worldviews of many U.S. Christians. The trending mindset reveals an entirely new form of normativity and permeates many aspects of *American* evangelical life. If left unchecked and unexamined, musical hegemony across the country will continue to dominate churches and Christian colleges and continue to alienate people of color who share faith in Jesus.

Notes

1. Lamott, Anne. *Traveling mercies: Some thought on faith.* New York, NY: Knopf Doubleday Publishing Group, 2000, p. 65.
2. Ibid., p. 42.
3. Rah, Soong-Chan. *The next evangelicalism: Releasing the church from Western cultural captivity: Easyread super large 18pt edition.* ReadHowYouWant.com, 2009.
4. Ibid.
5. Chang, Hyun Kyong. *Musical encounters in Korean Christianity: A trans-Pacific narrative.* 2014. University of California, Los Angeles, Ph.D. dissertation.
6. Hyaeweol Choi. *Gender and mission encounters in Korea: New women, old ways.* Berkeley, CA and Los Angeles, CA: University of California Press, 2009, and Wells, Kenneth. *New God, new nation: Protestants and self-reconstruction nationalism in Korea, 1896–1937.* Honolulu, HI: University of Hawai'i Press, 1990.
7. Rogal, Samuel J. *A general introduction to hymnody and congregational song.* Metuchen: The American Theological Library Association and The Scarecrow Press, Inc., 1991.
8. Ibid., pp. 22–23.
9. Luther, Martin. *Luther's works, vol. 40, church and ministry II.* ed. Congrad Bergendoff, gen. ed. Halmut T. Lehmann. Philadelphia, PA: Muhlenberg Press, 1958, p. 300.
10. Althaus, Paul. *The theology of Martin Luther.* Minneapolis, MN: Fortress Press, 1966.

11. F. Benson, Louis. *The hymnody of the Christian church*. Richmond, VA: John Knox Press, 1960, p. 75.

12. Maultsby, Portia K. "The Use and Performance of Hymnody, Spirituals, and Gospels in the Black Church," *The Western Journal of Black Studies* 7(3): 161–170, 1983.

13. Ibid.

14. Spencer, Jon Michael. "Black Denominational Hymnody and Growth Toward Religious and Racial Maturity," *Hymn* 41: 44, 1990.

15. Ibid., p. 45.

16. Isasi-Diaz, Ada Maria. "By the Rivers of Babylon: Exile as a Way of Life." In *Reading from this place.*, edited by Fernando F. Segovia and Mary Ann Tolbert. Minneapolis, MN: Fortress Press, 1990, p. 159.

17. Ibid., p. 156.

18. Ibid., p. 157.

19. Brueggemann, Walter. *The message of the psalms: A theological commentary*. Minneapolis, MN: Augsburg, 1984, p. 26.

20. Ibid., p. 27.

21. Berger, Peter. *The sacred canopy: Elements of a sociological theory of religion*. New York, NY: Anchor Books, 1968, p. 59.

22. Ibid., p. 55.

23. McCutchan, Stephen. "Illuminating the Dark: Using the Psalms of Lament," *Christian Ministry* 24: 14, 1993.

24. Walker, Alice. The Color Purple. Orlando, FL: Harcourt, Inc, 1982, p. 187.

25. "Litany at Atlanta." In *The seventh son: The thought and writings of W. E. B. Du Bois*, vol. 1, edited by Julius Lester. New York, NY: Random House, 1971, p. 425.

26. Carter, Joe. *Debatable: Is Christian Hip Hop Ungodly?* The Gospel Coalition, December 2013. Retrieved https://www.thegospelcoalition.org/article/debatable-is-christian-hip-hop-ungodly.

27. Ellis, Carl, and Karen Ellis. "A Letter to Our Young Brothers and Sisters," November, 2013. Retrieved from http://drcarlellisjr.blogspot.com/2013/11/a-letter-to-young-brothers-and-sisters.html

28. Paredes-Collins, Kristin. "Cultivating Diversity and Spirituality: A Compelling Interest for Institutional Priority," *Christian Higher Education* 12(1/2): 122–137, 2013. doi:10.1080/15363759.2013.739436.

29. Ash, Allison. N., and Laurie. A. Schreiner. "Pathways to Success for Students of Color in Christian Colleges: The Role of Institutional Integrity and Sense of Community," *Christian Higher Education* 15(1–2): 38–61, 2016. doi:10.1080/15363759/2015.1106356.

30. Edwards, Korie L. *The elusive dream: The power of race in interracial churches*. New York, NY: Oxford University Press, 2008, p. vii.

31. Ibid., p. 6.

· 8 ·

BEFORE JESUS BECAME WHITE

You have a fine way of rejecting the commandment of God in order to keep your tradition!

—Jesus (Mark 7:9)

Reclaiming a Biblical Vision of Justice

The Gospels—the four accounts of Jesus' life, ministry, death, and resurrection—characteristically portray Jesus keeping company with people the religious and political leaders of the time considered unworthy of association and/or socially unacceptable. Practicing a *table theology*,[1] Jesus regularly eats meals with people from diverse and often oppositional sociocultural backgrounds. By exhibiting a radical ethic of openness, Jesus in each narrative turns toward the humanity of people that the society despises, marginalizes, and disposes through systems of religious and political power. In this chapter, we strive to reclaim the biblical vision of justice embedded in the biblical witness as essential to understanding Jesus' calling and what it means to follow him. We highlight several key passages to emphasize the importance of cultivating the kind of table disposition and ethics Jesus practiced in his life and ministry. The book of Luke, for example, contains at least ten examples of table meals during which Jesus breaches sociopolitical boundaries and religious ritual.[2] Stories emphasizing how Jesus, as a matter of practice, communes with people whom those in power considered off limits, reveal something significant about his mission: Jesus repeatedly sought kinship and solidarity with rejected people. This chapter explores a vision of justice in the biblical witness to reclaim knowledge about Jesus before he became White. In doing so, we refute any rhetoric, policies, and practices that appropriate the name and person of Jesus to secure and maintain xenophobic, militarized, violent American imperialist, settler colonialist, heteropatriarchal capitalist, and White supremacist agendas and power.

Consider a vivid account in the book of Luke, chapter five, when Jesus invites a tax collector, Levi, to eat with him. As a tax collector in the ancient world, Levi would have been tasked with paying advanced taxes and assessing levies on the Jewish population to reimburse himself and his expenses. This kind of arrangement left room for unmitigated corruption. Levi could easily collect as much money as possible and turn a profit from the system, a practice the people would have known occurred among most tax collectors. Therefore, when Jesus holds a banquet at Levi's house with tax collectors and other sinners, the moment is contemptable. By sharing a meal with objectionable people like tax collectors, Jesus embodies an important message: He has come to call sinners, not the righteous, to repent. In response to the critiques of religious leaders, who disdain his willingness to engage in such loathsome behavior, Jesus replies (in Matthew 9:13), "Go and learn what this means, I desire mercy not sacrifice." By inviting the religious authorities to learn "what this means," Jesus pronounces the disintegration of religious purity laws, which function in exclusionary ways. The Gospels show Jesus touching the sick, dining with outcasts, and performing acts of solidarity that violate religious law and precede purification.[3] In doing so, Jesus' disposition and ethics reveal a biblical vision of justice that the White architecture of salvation conceals. The righteous are not the ones we expect.

The numerous examples of Jesus sanctioning meals with socially unacceptable people help to enflesh a biblical vision of justice that induces a *table mindset and ethics* that invite people to lovingly and openly turn toward God and one another. In an inversion of social arrangements, Jesus' *table mindset and ethics* encourage face-to-face interactions among contested groups. Food, while a necessity, is also enjoyable. Just the right amount of physical food can shift dispositions and power arrangements in ways that not only open minds and hearts, but also catalyze spiritual imagination that envisions the *kindom* of

God "on earth as it is in heaven" (sometimes we use *kindom* as a term to express how God's people come together, while other times we use the monarchical metaphor *kingdom* that is used in the Bible). Jesus' interactions with socially rejected and disposable people, especially at the hands of the powerful (political and/or religious), convey important lessons. Glimpsing the *kindom* of God not only produces fulfillment and joy, but repentance—especially among those working to defend their religious dominance.

This chapter will explore a *table theology and ethics* through interpretations of specific biblical readings that illustrate a commitment (in interpretation and action) to racial justice that reclaims Jesus of the Gospels from the forces of White supremacy. While persons already familiar with the biblical narratives may find the chapter accessible and easy to read, we hope the examples are also relevant to persons unfamiliar with them. We believe that making visible the logic and practices that distort what we know about Jesus helps us to recapture a biblical vision of Jesus as a champion for justice who calls his followers to imitate him by going to the people and places he went at the margins of society. In doing so, God liberates people and society.

The Radical Vision of Jesus' Open Table

Three essential narratives in scripture will serve as the body of the chapter. While we do not exegete specific passages involving Jesus at the meal table, we interpret key biblical stories that illustrate the radical vision of *open table* that Jesus modeled in his life, ministry, death, and resurrection. The first set of stories involve the Tower of Babel in the Hebrew Bible, specifically Genesis, chapter 11, and the event of Pentecost in Acts, chapter two. Juxtaposing key narratives in Genesis and Acts will addresses how interpreters misuse the story of Babel to show that God scatters people and languages, thus creating diversity, as a judgment against people trying become like God. In Acts, chapter two, the Pentecost event demonstrates how the Spirit of God works in linguistic differences and reconciles the conundrum at Babel. In fact, the two passages work together as bookends in a powerful way to reveal that diversity should not be understood as divine punishment, but rather, a *gift* from God. The second set of stories in Mark, chapters four and five, show Jesus taking his followers to societies outside their comfort zones and ultimately leading them to a catalytic scene of Jesus healing a troubled man. The third and final passage comes from the Gospel according to John, chapter 21, when Jesus appears to his followers after his resurrection from death. Jesus confronts his closest follower, who has resorted back to his old life and habits, which led to old routines and rhetoric. The combination of passages reveals how Jesus, the progenitor of divine justice, repossesses creation in ways that ignite systemic and individual liberation. By reclaiming Jesus before he was White, we call attention to the *kindom* disposition, ethics, and power Jesus revealed. People and institutions that seek to preserve their own interests by appropriating Jesus through a counterfeit White Jesus dehumanize people on the margins of society, distort their own humanity, renounce the gospel, and mock the love and justice of God that liberates and gives life to the cosmos.

The Tower of Babel

The Tower of Babel in Genesis 11 is a story about the complex reality of a world that has become characterized by childlike renderings of the Bible (i.e., books and Sunday school curriculum that depict a simplistic people trying to physically reach God with a tower). The people construct a tower with the intent of reaching the heavens and gaining equality with God. In the story, God punishes the people by making their ability to communicate and understand one another impossible. They now speak different languages. In the preceding chapters, Genesis 9 and 10, there is a similar theme of the people spreading out. However, spreading out here is not associated with the judgment and punishment chapter 11 denotes. In fact, Genesis, chapter 10, contains several neutral examples of the verb, to *spread*, as seen in the following examples: "from these coastlines, people spread" (Genesis 10:5); "the families of the Canaanites spread abroad" (Genesis 10:18); "these are the descendants of Ham by their families, their languages, their lands, and their nations" (Genesis 10:20); "these are the descendants of Shem by their families, their languages, their lands, and their nations" (Genesis 10:31); "these are the families of Noah's sons according to their genealogies and their nations" (Genesis 10:32). Genesis 10 does not automatically equate *spreading out* with judgment and punishment.

Genesis Chapter 11 declares that the whole earth had one language and used the same words. And as they migrated from the East, the people came upon a plane in the land of Shinar and settled there. The people had an idea and said, "Come, let us make bricks and burn them thoroughly," and then they said, "Come, let us build ourselves a city and a tower with its top in the heavens and let us make a name for ourselves. Otherwise, we shall be scattered abroad upon the face of the whole earth" (Genesis 11:3–4). The story assumes a universal posture in speaking about the whole earth, and the passages explore the themes of unity and diversity. Then "the Lord came down to see the city and the tower, which the mortals had built, and said, 'Look, they are one people and they all have one language and this is only the beginning of what they will do. Nothing that they propose to do will be impossible for them. Come, let us go down and confuse their language there so they will not understand one another's speech'" (Genesis 11:5–6). So, the Lord scattered them abroad, there and over the face of the earth, and they left off building the city. What the people had been doing willingly in chapter 10 (spreading), they stopped doing to gain power through unity. As a result, God commanded their spreading by confusing their languages. Therefore, the Tower of Babel represents how God confused the languages of all people and spread them broadly across the face of the earth. There are multiple ways to interpret the act of scattering, but Brueggemann notes that human unity is a complex reality in the text.[4] Unity is typically considered part of God's will, something humanity desires. In this case, unity stands against God's will because it is more about self-preservation and the power of domination, perhaps connected to the idea that those who seek to save their own lives will lose them.

The notions of *uniformity* and *unity* may contain an important nuance for this particular reading. Consider how diversity, unity, and languages are rendered in Acts, a companion book to Luke, which chronicles the life of the early Christian church in the first century. Acts two specifically recounts Pentecost, an event that takes place during the Jewish *Feast of Weeks* when the Holy Spirit descends upon the Jesus' closest followers and grants them special abilities to communicate across different languages. Despite humankind's failed attempt to gain equality with God by building the Tower of Babel, the Spirit of God descends upon the followers of Jesus. The impartation of God's Spirit to humankind is what ultimately reconciles ethnically and linguistically diverse social groups one to another. Interpreters often pair the scenes of Pentecost and the Tower of Babel to demonstrate the idea that God is reversing positions on diversity and uniformity. Acts, chapter two, however, shows that reconciliation occurs through people understanding one another's diverse languages and not replicating the uniformity that came before Babel. Humanity retains linguistic distinctions after Babel. That everyone *heard* the gospel in their own languages shows that it was not just in the apostles' *speaking* that language barriers were transcended—but in *hearing* and *understanding* people in their native languages. In Acts, chapter two, the Spirit of God preserves linguistic diversity at Pentecost. Rather than erasing linguistic multiplicity, Pentecost shows how the Spirit of God enables people across languages and cultures to hear and understand one gospel, which is considered universal and for all people and the entire creation. Amazed and astonished, the people at the Pentecost ask, "Are not all these who are speaking Galileans? And how is it that we hear each of us in our own native language?" (Acts 2:8). In Acts 2:11, they proclaim, "our languages, we hear them speaking about God's deeds of power." If Babel had been a punishment to overcome, the Spirit could have fostered unity through the obliteration of difference. Instead, the differences Babel established remain in Jerusalem. What the Spirit erased was division among the people because of their differences. They could now finally understand one another *in* their diversity. The diversity of language is not a problem to overcome. Instead, it is a blessing God pours out, a gift to be received. Linguistic distinctions enrich human understanding of the world and God. After all, God, not humankind, created diversity.

Biblical unity is not the erasure of difference, but rather, the capacity to live together without oppression and in tune with God's purposes for the world. Uniformity and domination cannot achieve unity for the Christian. The Spirit is not a personal gift from God for individuals and institutions to privatize and leverage for self-interested benefit. Rather, through the work of the Spirit appearing at Pentecost, God sanctions belonging, inclusion, and justice.

Acts, chapter two, verse 42 shows how the followers of Jesus devoted themselves to the apostles' teaching, to living in solidarity and mutuality, and to the breaking of bread. The acts and signs of the apostles produced awe; all who believed were together and had *all things in common*. In verse 45, the people sold their possessions and goods and distributed the proceeds to any who had need. They spent much time together and joyfully ate their food, praising God, and sharing goodwill with all people. Acts records the norms of faith in Jesus as sharing, teaching, fellowship, breaking bread, and prayer, and emphasizes these practices throughout the book. Having all things in common refers to friendship, beliefs, core values, and communal well-being.

The biblical pattern of selling property, distributing proceeds to reflect the social character of God's kingdom, and sharing equally in the good gifts of God is understood in the Hebrew Bible as *jubilee*, which the Israelites practice. The community in Acts shares its resources in ways that are similar to the practices of jubilee among the Israelites. In Acts, teaching, building community, sharing goods, and prayers are the ritual practices among those who repent and assent to the faith. Keeping the practices is impossible without the Spirit of God and the habits of a repentant mind and purified heart. They are too demanding for an individual believer. The images of kinship in Acts are communal in nature and involve shared goods, resources, and spiritual practices.

The parallels and contrast of Babel and Pentecost are worth remembering. In Jerusalem at Pentecost, the people gathered in one place, like Shinar, and the concern was not about being scattered. Instead, it was perhaps about people losing their lives and their power. In Acts, the people are not working to make a name for themselves. They are proclaiming the power of God. In Babel, they are reaching *up* to pierce the heavens in homogeneity, and they use their uniformity as a means to establish self-serving power. At Pentecost, the Spirit of God is poured *down* upon living beings, and their diversity is a means of achieving unity of purpose and the proclamation of a selfless gospel. Babel aims toward unity through uniformity, while Pentecost establishes community in diversity. At Pentecost, the Spirit gave everyone a voice, and they maintained the distinctions of their native languages. Hearing and understanding through the power of the Spirit led to a stable system of distributed justice. There were no extra regulations or requirements. There was no rule or universal law; the Spirit filled each person and gave life to the community.

In the contemporary context of White dominance and racism, the stories of Babel and Pentecost are important reminders about the dangers of homogeneity in reproducing domination. They also reveal the importance of diversity in striving for unity. Babel teaches about the hazards of groups that seek to remain insular and become powerful while suppressing others' humanity. Pentecost shows that diversity, which had its inception at Babel, was meant to be preserved. Volf has written that culture clashes with culture and justice struggles against justice, but people need inspiration from Acts as reminders that the impossible is possible; submerged voices will prophesy boldly and closed eyes can be opened with visions.[5] When understood in light of Volf's interpretation, the story of Acts can point people to a better interpretation of the Tower of Babel by reminding them that the impossible is possible through the unifying work of the Spirit. There is tension over unity, uniformity, and diversity. Babel and Pentecost ultimately show how sharing a table and life together in the kinship of the Spirit—even in the absence of a shared language—reveals deep insights not only about unity and diversity, but the character of God.

⁓ Demons on the Other Side

There are several indications that the followers of Jesus were subject to the temptations of exclusivity and power—the same corruptions that Jesus criticized. In one example, Jesus and his followers had gotten away from the crowds and towns to the beautiful region of Tyre and Sidon. While taking a break, an outsider (this time a Canaanite woman) came and pleaded with Jesus to help her daughter. A woman and an outsider, the Canaanite woman is doubly minoritized in this setting. The followers of Jesus quickly ask him to get rid of her, claiming that she was coming after them, despite that she only asked for one person—Jesus. In a perplexing turn of events, Jesus ignores and rejects her, and then rejects her more fiercely, comparing her to a dog. Jesus' rejections are uncharacteristic, and none of them seem to faze her. In a quick turn-around, Jesus praises her faith and heals her daughter. Perhaps the best way to understand this passage is by recognizing that Jesus was not teaching or testing the woman. Instead, Jesus was mirroring the exclusive and elitist ways of his closest followers. Jesus offers a parable and declares, whatever you *did* or *did not* do for the *least* of the brothers and sisters, you *did* or *did not* do for Jesus. If Jesus meant what he said or intended for his words to be taken literally, Jesus' ethics in the story of the Canaanite woman cannot be ignored. Jesus reveals the immorality and injustice of exclusionary and elitist practices and subverts the conventional norms of respectability. Jesus opens tables that are supposed to remain closed to people whose humanity the law treats as irredeemable.

Another poignant example in the book of Mark, chapter five, is the story of Jesus healing a "demon-possessed" man. This story is particularly interesting because it shows Jesus' desire to engage with people who are disenfranchised, contaminated, and outcasts in society. In the passage, Jesus and his followers have come to the other side of the Sea of Galilee to the country of the Gerasenes. As with other spatial/geographical notes in the Bible, this particular clue is important. The side where they begin, the West side of the Sea of Galilee, is their home base. Geographically, this territory provides some cultural comfort since Jewish people reside there. It is where Jesus' followers grew up, and it is the culture they know. The place is marked by people who are religiously astute. They maintain the appropriate behaviors of cleanliness, ritual washing, worshipping, eating, etc. In colloquial terms, going to the other side of the sea (East) would be going to the *wrong side of the tracks* for folks holding normative cultural power. Not only is the setting geographically opposite, it is also where people do not understand how to be proper, how to know God, how to be civilized. It is possible that Jesus' disciples, who demonstrate in several places that they do not appreciate being around people who are not like them, are not pleased to have travelled so far away from their home to an unfamiliar, uncivilized place. In fact, this passage is the first recording of Jesus travelling to the East side of the Sea of Galilee.

Jesus and his followers travel by boat. Upon getting to the other side of the sea, the passage says that Jesus immediately stepped out of the boat and a man with an unclean Spirit came out of the tombs to meet him. What is unclean about the man becomes clearer as the reader learns that he had been restrained with chains and broke them. No one had the strength to subdue him. The man lived among the tombs and in the mountains, always howling and bruising himself with stones. When the demon-possessed man approaches Jesus, Jesus heals him. This healing frightened the people who witnessed it. They asked Jesus to leave, but the man begged to go with the visitors from the boat. Jesus refused and said, "Go home to your friends and tell them how much the Lord has done for you and what mercy he has shown you" (Mark 5:19). The man went away and proclaimed his healing all around the region of the ten cities on the East side of the Sea of Galilee.

Jesus and his followers had only been there a very short time and then immediately went back to a place that felt more comfortable—the West side. Jesus was still very popular and had many Jewish followers. Huge crowds followed him and listened to him speak for great lengths of time. At one point, Jesus became concerned with how long a group of people had been with him. In an attempt to nourish them physically, Jesus collected five loaves and two fish. He ordered them to get all the people into groups and to sit on the grass. He divided the small amount of food and fed the entire crowd of thousands of people until they were full. This act is considered a miracle, showing a multiplication to provide for basic needs—food. There was so much food that the disciples took up *12 baskets* full of broken pieces as leftovers. Those who had eaten the loaves numbered 5,000. In addition to geography, numbers often have significance in the biblical text, as evidenced in the number of baskets of food. As the disciples collected 12 baskets full of broken pieces of fish, Jesus offered not only physical nourishment, not just food, but Spiritual nourishment, Spiritual teaching, and Spiritual food. The 12 baskets signify that on the West side of the Sea of Galilee, the food is left for the 12 tribes of Israel—the people who are considered knowledgeable, proper, and on the inside of a right relationship with God. They are the chosen ones—God's people.

The significance of the demon on the "other side" comes full circle when Jesus and some of his followers later returned to the East side. This is the *second* time that they cross the Sea of Galilee. Even though Jesus is only showing up for the second time in Mark 8, there was a great crowd waiting to listen to his teaching. After many hours without anything to eat, Jesus says, "I have compassion for this crowd because they have been with me now and they have nothing to eat. If I send them away hungry, they will faint on the way home and some of them have come a great distance" (Mark 8:2). The disciples reply, "How can one feed these people with bread here in the desert?" (Mark 8:4). They convey an even more negative tone than when they responded to Jesus feeding people on the West side of the Sea of Galilee, since they are now in the desert. The place is isolated, desolate, and far from home in many ways.

This time, Jesus collects 7 loaves and a few small fish and feeds an entire crowd of 4,000 until they were full; then, they take up the broken pieces left over. There were *seven baskets that were full*. Instead of 12 baskets, on the East side of the Sea of Galilee, there were seven baskets. In the same vein of numerical significance, seven is a number that represents completion or perfection. If the message for the West side of the Sea of Galilee was for the 12 tribes of Israel, perhaps the message on the East side implies that if the kingdom of God is to grow and become complete, it must engage beyond what is familiar and normative. The gospel must be taken beyond the places and people who have been perceived to be deserving or proper. When Jesus performed the same miracle on the East side as he did on the West—only with a different result (i.e., 7 baskets)—the miracle represented completion. Jesus obliterated the perceptions about who should be classified as deserving or proper. He challenged the disciples and others who preferred comfortable cultural norms. It was only in this new reality that the gospel was fully complete. Jesus provided nourishment in a communal space that disrupted the insider/outsider status. This powerful act served to dismantle perceptions about who stood outside of God's favor.

The story of Jesus feeding the masses—physically and Spiritually—has a unique connection to *table theology and ethics*. The opposition to breaking comfort zones, eating with disenfranchised people, and confronting persons who are considered to be possessed by demons will come in many forms. Whether asking the outsiders to leave or claiming there is no food in isolated deserts, the arguments against following Jesus to fulfill the gospel message will always be fierce and consistent. Demonizing people perceived to be on the

other side is certainly an enduring strategy, but Jesus sets a compelling example of crossing over to dismantle the ideals about who is in, who is out, or who
is considered untouchable.

Do You Love Me?

Jesus was executed through state-sanctioned violence in some combination of
religious and political power. The scandal of Jesus' execution occurred when
he returned from the grave in the resurrection. A series of Jesus' appearances
after his death culminated in an encounter with one of the disciples in John
21. This represents the tendency for Jesus' followers to act from old habits,
motivations, and their own human nature rather than from the calling to
be a follower of Jesus. To fully comprehend the encounter in John 21, which
involves a powerful dialogue between Jesus and Peter, it is critical to understand Peter's disposition before Jesus was executed.

Peter is a disciple who followed Jesus. However, Jesus predicted that Peter
would deny him three times during the process of his execution. This prediction becomes a reality when Peter is standing over a charcoal fire warming
himself and is questioned as to whether he is a follower of Jesus. This scene
is the first time a charcoal fire is mentioned in the New Testament, a detail
that becomes important later in the story. At this moment, Peter denied his
affiliation with Jesus, which was the third time he had denied Jesus that night.
Jesus' prediction had become true. Upon that third denial, a rooster crowed.
Jesus was sentenced to death and was executed on a Roman cross.

A look back in Peter and Jesus' relationship reveals that Jesus first met
Peter when he was fishing. Jesus had told Peter and his fellow fishermen to
cast their nets on the other side of their boat, which turned out to be a successful measure. After Jesus dies, Peter decides to permanently return to his
old life of fishing. Perhaps in Peter's mind, the ministry Jesus began had now
collapsed. It is fascinating that upon the apparent failure of the movement,
Peter so quickly abandons the cause. Because Peter is the consummate leader,
the other disciples commit to going with him. This passage is a reminder of
how easy it is to return to places of comfort. Deeply ingrained belief systems
must undergo severe reconstruction.

With Peter's return to fishing, it is logical that when Jesus returns from
death, Peter was fishing—exactly what he did before he came into contact
with Jesus. In a scene of immense replay, irony, and a night of fishing with no
success, Jesus says to the men in the boat, "Little boys, cast your nets on the

other side," the same command Jesus had given when he first met Peter and the other disciples. When Peter heard it was Jesus, he jumped into the sea, and then the other disciples followed with a boat dragging the net full of fish. Peter must have arrived to Jesus first after swimming to shore, but all of the disciples saw a charcoal fire there on the beach. Surely, the similar words Jesus used to instruct them to cast the nets on the other side of the boat, and the familiar scene of a charcoal fire, had a profound psychological and existential impact on Peter. The impact on Peter of being thrust back to these places of memory is hard to estimate. Peter likely experienced overwhelming guilt from having denied Jesus, someone he fiercely defended. It must have been con- victing to be presented with the details of his denial with smells and scenes of reverting back to his old ways. Peter was one of the followers to whom Jesus taught the same lessons of openness and inclusion over and over again. Peter's patterns of forgetfulness or resistance are not only present in Peter, but the disciples and human nature in general.

Jesus instructing the disciples about their fishing, the scene of the char- coal fire, and the disciples eating fish parallel many of the details that had been present at critical moments of Jesus and Peter's relationship before Jesus' death. All of these parallel details set the stage for the complex dia- logue that ensues between Jesus and Peter—a dialogue that reveals and con- fronts the role of change, guilt, revolution, and love in Peter. Jesus asks Peter, "Do you love me?" (John 21:15). There are times when concepts and vocab- ulary in the English translation of the Bible do not align with the meaning in the original language. In the original Greek language in which the New Testament was written, there are several words with different meanings that end up being translated into the same word *love* in English. When Jesus asks if Peter loved him, he says, "Do you *agapas* me?" This form of love is from the Greek root word *agape*, which makes the question mean, "Do you love me unconditionally?" Peter replies to him, "Yes, Lord, you know that I love you" (John 21: 15), but he does not use *agapas* in his response. Instead, he responds with, "You know, I *philo* you." Or, "you know I have a fondness for you." A second time, Jesus uses *agapas* and asks, "Do you love me?" (John 21:16), meaning an unconditional love. Peter again replies without using *agapas*, saying, "Yes, Lord, you know I'm very fond of you." A third time, Jesus asks but does not to use *agapas*. Instead, Jesus says, "Do you *phileis* me?" (John 21:17). In this instance, Jesus switches his words to match Peter's and to say, "Are you fond of me?" Peter is not catching on. He feels hurt because of the repeated question and exclaims, "Lord, you know everything." Essentially

Peter acknowledges that Jesus is omniscient and says, "You know that I *am very fond* you."

Peter's reverts to his old ways with guilt. He is mired in his own feelings of paralysis so that he cannot bring himself to tell Jesus that he loves him unconditionally. His entire being resists the love of Jesus. Peter denied Jesus three times before his death and has essentially denied his love three times in his resurrected appearance.

This story is perhaps one of the most powerful interactions between Jesus and another person recorded in biblical text. It reveals how human nature influences people to abandon the revolutionary path of Jesus—even the people who have previously chosen to follow the ways and teachings of Jesus. When the pressure was on, Peter denied ever having known Jesus at the most critical time in Jesus' life when he was about to be unjustly executed. Peter discarded the entire movement and reverted to his old life of fishing. In the end, Peter could not bring himself to confess his unconditional love for Jesus. Peter was more concerned about his own safety, comfort, and control than following Jesus and continuing the movement he started.

In reclaiming Jesus and the Gospel's architecture of salvation, Peter's rejection exposes the reality that human nature is self-interested and self-protective. It is normative to return to places of personal comfort. Peter—someone who spent close, intimate time with Jesus—was called a rock on which the Church was going to be built. A leader with the enormous influence of Peter may shed light on the human tendency to sustain self-protection and power, two features that sustain the social construction of White Jesus and the White architecture of salvation. Ironically in this story, Peter, one of Jesus' insiders, becomes the outcast. Jesus' table theology and ethics are evident when he reaches out to Peter and eats a meal with him at the same place (i.e., a charcoal fire) where Peter showed his greatest moment of betrayal. The theological significance here is that to follow Jesus, it truly requires following him to places where we avoid constructing Jesus or salvation in our own self-protecting image. No matter how close or far Jesus' followers have wandered, he calls them back to follow him and love others.

A Way Forward

Do you have eyes to see? The Bible is replete with examples of reconciliation: first God to the people, and second, people to one another. God reveals the plan to redeem the people, reconciling them to God and to one another through the Tower of Babel and Pentecost. God challenges the disciples to move past spaces of normativity and discomfort to establish new relationships with people they otherwise excluded. God reminds Peter to love others deeply as a sign of love for God. The Spirit of God in communal life makes this kind of love possible.

Notes

1. *Table theology* is a term used to indicate the ways in which we can know or understand God through the table experience and the record of the ways in which Jesus used a table to reveal a radical message of love and community.
2. Hicks, John Mark. *Come to the table: Revisioning the Lord's Supper.* Orange, CA: Leafwood Publishers, 2002.
3. Beck, Richard Allan. *Unclean: Meditations on purity, hospitality, and morality.* Eugene, OR: Cascade Books, 2011.
4. Brueggemann, Walter. *An introduction to the Old Testament: The canon and Christian imagination.* Louisville, KY: Westminster John Knox, 2012.
5. Volf, Miroslav. *Exclusion and embrace: A theological exploration of identity, otherness, and reconciliation.* Nashville, TN: Abingdon Press, 2008.

AFTERWORD

When we began this project, we were not certain where it would take us. We were certain, however, that some readers would feel defensive, threatened, or challenged by many of our positions. Our intent was not to be controversial, and we acknowledge that our understanding is limited and our perspectives are culturally bound. This has been a spiritual journey for each of us and we have bared our souls. To even write *White Jesus* felt uncomfortable or irreverent at times. Our tenacious self-searching and society-searching caused a tension within us as we tried to figure out the architectures, scapes, and flows of meaning. As we came to the end of the project, we felt a profound sense of discomfort with all that we had found—within us and around us. White Jesus is a myth and a socially constructed aberration of the true Jesus of Nazareth. However, the power fixed in this deviation found in White Jesus is real.

The brief compilation of events, concepts, images, and ideologies in this book shows the degree to which religious principles and justifications are culturally and contextually bound. Even timeless, eternal, and divine truths are filtered through temporal lenses, making the truth more difficult to understand. In discussions of White Jesus, we have found that the imagery can overtake the meaning of the historical and ideological apparatus. Here we include one more image and story to show the ways in which White Jesus is a combination of what we see and what we believe.

In the 1930s, Olvera Street in Los Angeles had effectively been purchased and was undergoing a renovation to make it appear like a stereotypical Mexican village. The purpose for the renovation was to appropriate a cultural essence in order to generate tourism. In 1932, muralist David Alfaro Siqueiros was commissioned to paint a mural above Olvera Street. Living and working for almost seven months in Los Angeles, the Mexican artist and revolutionary worked to complete the commission of painting something tropical. The resulting mural, *América Tropical*, was unveiled to the woman who made the commission and a group of Los Angeles elites in an event that scandalized many of the attendees.

The painting shows indigenous Mexican revolutionaries and an indigenous brown body hanging on a cross overlooked by an imperial American eagle. Almost immediately after the unveiling, the mural was whitewashed (though somewhat ineffectively), and Siqueiros was deported following the expiration of his visa. A more thorough whitewashing effort occurred shortly thereafter.

The mural was rediscovered in the 1960s. After an ambitious and lengthy project by the Getty Conservation Institute, the mural was conserved so that the original painting was revealed. There is a small museum explaining the events that took place and the social significance. A viewing deck allows visitors to see the original mural. The picture shown here was taken with a group of our doctoral students who took the train into Los Angeles for an afternoon experience. As a small group gazing quietly upon this work of art, this spiritual and political image of the cross that had twice been whitewashed, it was not lost on us that indigenous Mexicans are some of the most oppressed peoples in Central and South America and now, by extension, so are Mexicans in the U.S.

People have obsessed over the question of whether or not Jesus was White. The scientific approach has garnered significant attention to the question as forensic experts have taken Semitic skulls and characteristics to recreate an image, while others have taken images from the Shroud of Turin to develop an image of Jesus. While this historical quest is interesting, as we have shown in this book, it does not unravel the myth, influence, and reality of White Jesus. The blend of the image and the concept has a historically rooted gravity that will take a long time to unravel.

In the book of Exodus, chapter 20, where the famous Ten Commandments are inscribed, God tells Moses in the second commandment:

Figure A.1: From a Viewing Platform, a Snapshot of the Mural, *América Tropical*, by David Alfaro Siqueiros.
Photo Credit: Christopher S. Collins.

> You shall not make for yourself an image in the form of anything in heaven above or on the earth beneath or in the waters below. You shall not bow down to them or worship them; for I, the Lord your God, am a jealous God, punishing the children for the sin of the parents to the third and fourth generation of those who hate me, but showing love to a thousand generations of those who love me and keep my commandments. (Exodus 20:4)

The idea of a White Jesus in America is a violation of the second commandment in the Decalogue. Human beings, made in God's own image, have distorted the image of God by creating their own. The purpose of this book was to demystify and interrogate the social construction of White Jesus and challenge our colleagues, churches, and Christian institutions to do the same.

To the question, was Jesus White, we can emphatically answer, no. To the question, has Jesus been made to be White, we answer yes, because under a sacred canopy, centuries of oppressive policies, hierarchies, and dispositions have been reinforced with a divine sense of supremacy. The short case studies and historical examples in this volume depict key moments in time and significant ideologies that serve to reinforce socially constructed dominance. As people of faith, we see this long history of aberration as offensive, and even sinful. Any discomfort we felt at the beginning was replaced with a deep sense of discomfort at the collection of evidence we found—within us and around us. Dismantling White supremacy must absolutely involve an in-depth look at religion and faith. Our religion and faith demand dismantling supremacy in all forms and all places.

As we reflect on this writing project, we remember all those who came before us. We lament with the countless numbers of people of color who suffered unnecessarily as a result of White supremacy and dominance in the name of Jesus in churches and societies across the globe. We also regret how this dominance has harmed White people—creating a false sense of superiority that distorts the image of God and creation. Finally, we mourn our own complicity in perpetuating and internalizing the White dominance that resides within each one of us. We are complicit in both our silence and at times our active engagement in the system that has benefitted us in myriad ways. For all of these reasons, we confess, and ask for forgiveness. We long to be better. We have learned a great deal from this project, and perhaps what we have learned most is that we continue to have many limitations and flaws that we cannot recognize in ourselves. We trust that those who come after us will recognize our efforts to humbly acknowledge our own brokenness.

INDEX

A

adoption, adopt, 41, 55, 62–68
    transracial, 62
African Methodist Episcopal, xxi, 10
America(n), United States of, xv, 3–4,
    7–13, 17–24, 29–33, 36–37, 41–45, 57,
    72–73, 76–77, 86, 91, 97, 114
Anabaptist, 27, 96
Angelou, Maya, xiii

B

baptized, xv, xiv, 20, 27
Barmen Declaration, 26
Barth, Karl, 26
Bellah, Robert, 24, 27
Birth of a Nation, 34–36
Black
    Church, xiv, 78, 91–92
    Christian(ity), 10, 42, 91–92
    Congregations, 90
    Gospel, 79
    Jesus, 9–10
Black Lives Matter, 47
Bob Jones University, 48, 77
Brueggemann, Walter, 93, 103
Bush, George W., 17

C

Camp, Lee C., 20
Catholic, xiii, 21, 27, 30,
    88–89
Charlottesville, 4, 34
Christian higher education, 8, 36–38,
    50–51, 71–79, 97
Christianity Today, 41, 45–46, 48, 50
Christian nation, 19, 24, 31, 43
Civil religion, xix, xx, 13, 17–20, 23–27,
    42–43
Civil War, xix, 9, 30–34, 73, 76

colonial(ism), 4, 10, 24, 37–38, 59, 62–63, 67–68, 73, 88, 95, 100
colorblind, 65–67
Cone, James, 1, 5, 9–10, 37
Constantine, xxi, 18, 20–21, 56
Constitution, 24, 59, 78
Council for Christian Colleges and Universities (CCCU), 72
Crosby, Fanny J., 88–89

D

Du Bois, W.E.B., 18, 31, 94
Duke Divinity School, 12–13

E

Edwards, Jonathan, 37–38
Edwards, Korie, 96
Enlightenment, xiii, 5–7, 23

F

Falwell, Jerry, 44, 77
Falwell Jr., Jerry, 43, 78

G

Gospel(s), xx, 1, 14, 18, 23, 25, 46, 67, 79, 81, 85, 95, 99–105, 108, 111
Graham, Billy, 44–46
Graham, Franklin, 43
Grudem, Wayne, 43

H

Ham, curse of, 22–23
Harlem Renaissance, 10–11
Holy Bible, 6, 17

Hughes, Langston, 11, 15
Hughes, Richard, 19–20

I

Imperialism, 9, 26, 56, 63, 87
Indian Boarding Schools, 19, 57, 60–62
Isasi-Diaz, Ada Maria, 93

J

Jefferson, Thomas, 11, 23–24
Bible, 23
Jennings, Willie, 72
Jones, Bob, 44

K

Kaepernick, Colin, 42
King, Rodney, 79
King Jr., Martin Luther, xii, 29, 46
Ku Klux Klan, 34

L

Lamott, Anne, 85
Liberty University, 43, 78
Luther, Martin, 45, 88

M

Malcolm X, 92
Marxism, 50, 81
McCutchan, Stephen, 94
Missionary, missionaries, 8, 13, 55–59, 63, 68, 74, 86–90, 96
Moore, Russell, 66–67
Moreland, J.P., 80

P

patriotism, xix, 18, 23–24, 26–27, 77
pentatonic scale, 86–88, 90–91, 94
Pentecost, 101, 103–105, 112
political marking, 50
political packaging, 50
Pratt, Richard Henry, 60–61
Presbyterian, xv, xvi, 33, 45, 73
Princeton Theological Seminary, xiii
Protestant(s), 21, 27, 36, 43–44, 59, 71–72, 77, 81, 87–88, 91

R

racism, racist, xx, 6, 8, 10, 13, 20–22, 24, 29–34, 36–38, 42, 44, 49–50, 64–66, 72–74, 79–82, 96
Rah, Soong-Chan, 75–76, 86
Reagan, Ronald, 47–48
religious right, 13, 42, 47–48, 50
religious White, 13, 41, 47, 50–52, 78
Republican Party, 8, 48, 78, 97

S

Salvation, xiiii, xv, xx, 1, 4–8, 19, 43, 45, 59, 62,
Sea of Galilee, 106–108
segregation, 9, 31–33, 37–38, 42, 45–47, 91
Siquerios, David Alfaro, 114–115
Stark, Rodney, 18

T

tax collector, 100
Tebow, Tim, 42
Tower of Babel, 101–105
Trump, Donald J., xi, 4, 8, 11, 43–44, 49, 78

W

Walker, Alice, 94
West, Cornel, xvi, 12
West, Western, 8–9, 30, 56, 81, 86–91, 94–95
    epistemology, 7
    European, 7–8, 89–90
    knowledge, 19
White,
    architecture of salvation, 1, 4–9, 11–12, 19–20, 31, 37, 42, 56, 58–59, 61, 63, 72, 78, 86, 92, 97, 100, 111
    Christians, 9–10, 13, 29–31, 33–34, 38, 42–44, 46–47, 61–62, 71, 73–77, 79, 81, 91, 96
    churches, 32, 38, 76, 92, 95
    dominance, 4–5, 12, 37–38, 56, 62, 72, 79, 86, 94, 105, 116
    evangelical Christian(ity), 1, 6, 41–47, 49, 77
    individualism, 45
    Jesus, xx-xxi, 1–4, 8–12, 18–19, 35, 42, 44, 52, 56, 61–62, 65, 67, 92, 102, 111, 113–115
    Privilege, 4, 42–43, 51, 80
    supremacy, xvi, xviii, xx, 1, 3–5, 10–13, 24, 29, 31–38, 42, 56, 60, 71–73, 79, 100–101, 115–116
    theology, 13, 36, 72–73, 75
    worship, 85–86, 91, 94
Williams, Jarvis, 79